# Living the Sweet Life

SIMPLE SECRETS TO FINDING PURPOSE,
JOY, AND FULFILLMENT EVERY DAY

# Living the Sweet Life

# RUTH JONES

For my husband, Llewellyn,
who makes every day sweeter than honey,
and for Aiden, my sweet life blessing.
I love you both so very much!

# Contents

# CONTENTS

*Eat honey, my son, for it is good;*
*honey from the comb is sweet to your taste.*
*Know also that wisdom is like honey for you:*
*If you find it, there is a future hope for you,*
*and your hope will not be cut off.*
*-Proverbs 24:13-14*

# Sweet Beginnings

There isn't a day that goes by that I don't remember what life was like before I lost her—the passionate dreamer I used to be. She was a woman who had a head full of stars and a heart full of fire.

I didn't lose her while shopping, like a mother whose child wanders off in the store aisles, but I had that same heart wrenching, pulse-pounding, can't-catch-your-breath panic the moment I realized *she's gone.*

I didn't know where she went. I didn't know when it happened. But she was gone without a trace.

Standing in the bathroom, hand over my mouth, tears running down my face, I gasped for breath as my mind reeled from the fresh realization that she was missing.

I had lost her… and I hadn't even noticed.

Whether she had vanished out of neglect, hid away out of resignation and disappointment, or simply been swept up in the undertow of the hustle and bustle of life…I don't know. But there was no doubt the bottom had fallen out of my heart and she was missing. Lost. Gone.

Looking in the mirror and I could no longer see my truest self. The inner child so full of wonder, spontaneity, and joy for life had wandered off and been replaced with a woman who was hurried and harried, frustrated and on fumes.

In those deep brown, tear-filled eyes staring back at me, I saw a woman who was exhausted, emotionally disconnected, and run down. I still had a vision for who God had called me to be, but my passion and motivation was on empty.

Somewhere along the way I had exchanged living for "making a living." It hadn't happened overnight, but my authentic self had retreated behind the safe and comfortable confines of a successful career, familiar routines, and the daily chaos of cooking family dinners, straightening toy-strewn rooms, and collapsing before Netflix. I had unknowingly traded in my deepest desires for a sweet life to the tyranny of the daily demand. I was busy as a bee but producing no honey.

My mind used to be so filled with ideas and adventures that I would fill up countless journals with dreams about my calling and promises ripe for pursuing. Now it was weighed down with worries about college funds and raging debates on whether to diet or just accept my baby-bearing, well deserved curves for what they were. I was overworked and under-joyed, missing the sweetness in the moments happening all around me.

As the bathroom closed in around me, I knew something had to change. If I continued my current pace, I would lose her for good. I had to find a way back to my authentic self—to the person God created me to be. I had to find a way to make the sweet life my way of life.

## The Quest Begins

That morning I resolved to begin a quest to find the things that make life sweet and to fully indulge in them. I read books and, like a scientist, I tested their hypotheses out in real-life situations. I had lengthy conversations with wise women, decades older than myself, asking them for the advice they'd wish they'd had at my age. I began realigning my priorities with the things that tugged on my heartstrings and awakened my soul.

Then one day, it all fell into place.

With my Bible in my lap, I was leaning into God, asking Him what the sweet kind of life He had designed for me was all about. Faintly, but clearly, He led me to Proverbs 24:13-14:

*"Eat honey, my son, for it is good; honey from the comb is sweet to your taste. Know also that wisdom is like honey for you: If you find it, there is a future hope for you, and your hope will not be cut off."*

Those eye-opening verses were a discovery that is the linchpin of this book: **The sweet life comes as the result of applying God's wisdom to your life every day. When you do, you can expect a future and a hope.**

When I began applying the wisdom from God's Word into my everyday situations, my life took on greater meaning and clarity. My mindset shifted from chasing milestones to enjoying moments. My passions came alive again, and I felt like I had more energy, more peace, and more zeal. Creative ideas returned and I could once again see countless ways to apply God's wisdom and accomplish the dreams He placed in me.

Over the years I refined this wisdom into practical strategies, well-worn habits and real, workable solutions—omitting ones that seemed good in theory but didn't work well in real life and adding others that simplified steps.

As I was working on experiencing a better life, God led me to others who also felt overworked and under-joyed. I began sharing the principles that transformed my life, and they put them into practice, achieving extraordinary results as well. Just from applying simple things like creating a personal space (Chapter 13) or giving themselves permission to downshift (Chapter 11), they reported feeling more alive, vibrant, and free. They shared stories of how they had become more self-aware, creative, and purposeful. As they made changes to live life sweeter, they began to positively influence and uplift their family members, their children, and even their community.

Hearing these stories of transformation filled me with even greater fervor. I wanted everyone to live what I was now calling *the* "Sweet Life"—a life that is vibrant, joy-filled, and filled with God's passion. I decided to do something about it and capture the wisdom secrets God had shown me all in one place.

*Living the Sweet Life* is that book. Each chapter unfolds wise secrets to living with more joy, fulfillment, passion, and appreciation that will transform ordinary moments into extraordinary experiences.

## What Makes This Book Different

A lot of conventional, self-help books focus on super-achievement through sheer willpower and discipline. This approach creates immense stress and frustration that often destroys motivation, damages relationships, and reduces creativity—delivering the opposite of everything promised. *Living the Sweet Life* makes the opposite claim. By leaning into God's wisdom and grace instead, you will make the progress you desire and be more imaginative, motivated, and altogether more fulfilled.

If you're feeling stuck, frustrated, listless, or bored, then *Living the Sweet Life* is for you. I'm here to give you hope and how-to's to living a life you love. My life's passion is to show you how to discover and claim the life you were meant to live. A full-to-overflowing, joyous, Sweet Life is your birthright.

Whether you're fresh out of college, entering the back half of life, or anything in between, the wisdom you'll find inside this book works. There is nothing magical about my Sweet Life, or how I got here. If you make the commitment to put these spiritual principles to practical use, you can join me in living a life of purpose and fulfillment, and I believe you'll be happier than you've been in a long time.

Sweet Life, here we come!

## Be Assured...

**1. You are starting at the perfect moment, in the perfect spot, to make life sweeter.**

Your current life may be the furthest thing from the life you envision. That's okay. Now is the perfect time to pivot and use the wisdom in the pages that follow. You were led to read this book at this exact moment for a reason. It's because you're ready. Follow your own north star back to the girl that's gone missing. You get to be the heroine in your own story—and it starts now.

**2. You don't need to stop everything or start over to have a Sweet Life every day.**

Believe it or not, I worked out the principles in *Living the Sweet Life* during busy years of career transition, starting a family, moving to a new state, losing a baby, changing careers, and launching a ministry—and not only did they work, but they helped me through it all. Your time-crunched schedule and life's inevitable ups and downs can only be enhanced by starting now, right where you are.

**3. You don't need to implement everything you're going to read all at once.**

Within *Living the Sweet Life,* you'll learn tips and techniques that you can savor a drop at a time. Simply work on one thing every day that will give you more joy, more peace, a deeper sense of meaning, and a greater feeling of connection. Practicing the principles of one chapter every day, or even one chapter every week, will help you develop positive habits that will make your life happier, easygoing, and fulfilled.

**4. You can read the book in any order.**

Outside of chapter one, each chapter in *Living the Sweet Life* is a self-contained bit of wisdom. Feel free to scan the table of contents and flip to the sweetness your heart needs the most. Toss this book in your gym bag, your purse, or desk drawer at work and pull it out whenever you need a tasty bit of goodness for your soul.

If you're ready to experience amazing energy and lead fulfilling days rediscovering your own Sweet Life, then buzz on to the next page and let's go!

xoxo,

*Ruth*

# Life Is Sweet

*Life is short, and it is up to you to make it sweet.*
*–Sarah Louise Delany*

⟨ BEE FACT ⟩

Honey is the only food that includes all the substances necessary to sustain life, including enzymes, vitamins, minerals, and water; and it's the only food that contains "pinocembrin," an antioxidant associated with improved brain functioning.

S our Patch Kids are the best candy. Ever. Eating them by the handful…even the bag-full…is the ultimate delight! They start off so sour and tart, but then, faster than you expect, they turn surprisingly sweet and fruity. There's nothing like that lip-puckering jolt. That's a fun experience from candy, but not from life. We all want to live the Sweet Life and avoid all the sour, bitter, and unexpected surprises if we can help it.

What does it mean to live the Sweet Life? Before we look at what it is, let's look at what it's *not*. Here are a few myths and mindsets that can easily derail your Sweet Life right from the start.

**The Sweet Life is not problem-free.** Life has its joys and sorrows, its mountaintops and valleys. What sets someone apart when living the Sweet Life is that they live with hope and an expectation for a positive future *despite* the pain of present trials.

**The Sweet Life isn't defined by pleasure, riches, success, or fame.** Hollywood proves these things don't guarantee happiness, peace, or meaningful fulfillment. While wealth, accomplishments, influence, and enjoyable experiences can certainly enhance life, they are neither the source nor the sustainer of the Sweet Life.

**The Sweet Life is not automatic. It's intentional, and it's a choice.** It's making a firm decision that you're not going to settle for the mediocre and the mundane, but instead choose to pursue God's best. The Sweet Life is an admission that you want *more*—more meaning, more joy, more freedom, more experience, more impact, and more fun! The Sweet Life is what you intentionally choose to make it, and it's within your reach.

**The Sweet Life is not cookie-cutter.** The Sweet Life is as unique as you are. It is composed of your dreams, passions, and priorities mixed with your special blend of education, skills, values and personality. My Sweet Life may not look like yours, and yours may not look like mine, or anyone else's. Use the Sweet Life of others for inspiration, but never for permission. That's incredibly freeing, isn't it? God created you unique, and He tailor-made your Sweet Life as a unique expression of His goodness toward you. You don't have to fit into any mold. He has divinely shaped who you are and what you love to lead you into the Sweet Life He has planned for you.

Now that you know what the Sweet Life is *not*, what exactly *is* it?

## The Sweet Life is...

Jesus revealed in John 10:10 the kind of experience He wants us to have: "I came that they may have *and* enjoy life, and have it in abundance [to the full, till it overflows]" (*AMP*).

God came to give you the Sweet Life. That's great news! Take a quick pause and do a fist pump in the air! God doesn't want you to live a humdrum life where you're just barely getting by. God wants to give you an enjoyable, boundless life.

Here are the four foundations of the Sweet Life:

**The Sweet Life is a fulfilled life.** It means you're living filled to the full! God came to give you a life full of peace, joy, and a zeal for living. He wants you to not only have a life, but also to enjoy it! He wants you to enjoy good health, meaningful work, satisfying experiences, and rich relationships with Him, your family, friends, and others. Your life should be fun! He wants you to enjoy life until you are so full you cannot possibly contain any more and you overflow—spilling over into everything and everyone around you.

The Sweet Life is lived in both the moments and the milestones. It's about finding the fulfilling parts of our lives, savoring them, and intentionally engaging in them.

**The Sweet Life is a fruitful life.** When people look at your life, they should see delicious fruit. That is, top-notch character and good works. When you're rocking the Sweet Life, you'll be making a difference in the lives of others and the world around you. Whether you're gathering neighborhood women for a small group, spearheading a nonprofit to teach sustainable farming on the other side of the

> That ye might walk worthy of the Lord unto all pleasing, being fruitful in every good work, and increasing in the knowledge of God.
> –Colossians 1:10

world, or raising godly kids in your own backyard, your heart is set on being fruitful wherever you're planted.

While you're cultivating a bumper crop of good works on

the outside, shoot down deep roots on the inside, and grow in the knowledge of God. Let God cultivate the rich fruit of His Spirit within you so you're a basket of tasty goodness through and through. As you increase in your knowledge of God, you'll increase in your fruitfulness.

And remember this: While a fruitful life won't spare you from your share of challenges and storms, you can remain boldly confident knowing that you are deeply cared for by a loving God. He has equipped you to deal with whatever challenges come your way. A fruitful life is born out of a faithful life, so remain faithful to God and to what He has called you to do.

**The Sweet Life is a focused life.** A focused life starts with a God-centered, God-empowered vision for your life. It's living out who God created you to be and doing what He created you to do—*with passion*. A focused person lives on assignment with a strong sense of purpose and a heart open to possibilities.

> No, dear brothers and sisters, I have not achieved it, but I focus on this one thing: Forgetting the past and looking forward to what lies ahead, I press on to reach the end of the race and receive the heavenly prize for which God, through Christ Jesus, is calling us.
> –Philippians 3:14

If you've ever met someone who didn't know what to do with their life, squandered their time, or maybe had dreams but never got around to doing them, you know getting them focused is an exercise in futility and frustration. However, someone living a focused life exudes passion, drive, and determination with every fiber of their being. That's who God has called you to be.

Take time to define what's important in your life by writing down your dreams, goals, and an action plan to achieve them. Then ask God to align how you spend your time, energy, and resources with your written vision.

Don't allow an overcrowded schedule, daily distractions, or a lack of intentionality to keep you from living out your true priorities. God came to give you a focused life—a life where He places a burning passion within you, and you pursue it with laser-like focus.

**The Sweet Life is a finished life.** What will your legacy be? Will it be one of character, determination, perseverance, and faith? When you leave this life, will you be able to say, "God I have used everything—all my time, talent, resources, and opportunities—all You have given me for Your glory?" A finished life is a life of legacy, a testament of faithfulness to God

I have fought the good fight, I have finished the race, I have kept the faith.
–2 Timothy 4:7

and what He called You to do. In return, you will also see God's faithfulness to you, blessing you with dreams fulfilled, potential realized, and an impactful life lived.

At the end of a finished life, like Paul, you can boldly say, "I have fought the good fight, I have finished the race, I have kept the faith" (2 Timothy 4:7). And you can joyfully expect Him to respond, "Well done, good and faithful servant. Enter into the joy of your Lord" (Matthew 21:23, NKJV).

*You can live the Sweet Life!*

It starts now. It starts with choices—deciding that you're not going to settle for the mediocre and the mundane. For some, it means giving up apathy and starting to dream again, hope again, and move again—even if it's a little uncomfortable and painful at first. For others, it may mean reassessing priorities, focusing on what matters, and eliminating distractions.

If your days are not fulfilling, fruitful, focused, and finishing what you were placed here to do, then it's time to make a shift. Keep reading and together we'll explore ways you can intentionally pursue the Sweet Life. After all, the Sweet Life is a journey. It doesn't happen overnight, and it's not a destination you arrive at on this side of Heaven. It's a continual pursuit—pressing forward for the prize.

The Sweet Life is yours, and it's beckoning you forward, so go for it!

## Sweet Life Secrets

- The Sweet Life is not automatic. It's intentional, and it's a choice.

- God has authored the Sweet Life just for you and it's tailored to your dreams, experiences, background, passions, gifts, and talents.

- When you're rocking a fruitful life, you'll be making a difference in the lives of others and the world around you.

- God came to give you a focused life—a life where He places a burning passion within you, and you respond with laser-like focus.

- A finished life is one in which you look back and the legacy you leave is a testament of faithfulness to God and what He called you to do.

# Big Destiny,
# Small Directions

*Little strokes fell great oaks.*
*–Benjamin Franklin*

One pound of honey takes up to 40,000 miles of flying to produce.

I started writing today knowing I only had about 90 minutes to write while my son was grabbing a quick nap. Usually I like to write when I have about three to four hours, so I can get in my flow and lose myself in my writing. However, I knew today that wouldn't be the case, and I would have to seize the moment and pen what I could. But just as I was contemplating firing up my laptop that insidious voice of perfectionism raised its head and whispered, "It's not worth it. You'll only finish one page at best. Wait until you have the time you "really need" to accomplish what you really want." Isn't that what happens to us all? The minute we try to make progress, the voices in our head try to talk us out of it. Last time I checked, accomplishing something trumps accomplishing nothing any day. Slow progress is better than no progress!

I have this big huge dream of writing lots of books that impact people and change their lives. And I see myself one day opening the mailbox or reading my email or social media and receiving a note from someone saying that my book was the difference maker in their life and somehow God used what I wrote to be the miracle they needed. Big dream right? But in order to accomplish that, my instructions are quite small. Show up every day and write. Not think about writing. Not do endless research. Not daydream about book signings and book tours. WRITE! Small and simple. But far from easy.

We all have big dreams, high hopes, and grand plans. God created you with a big destiny in mind. You are chosen to do great, big, world-changing, culture-shattering, life-giving, audacious things. But big destinies come packaged with small instructions.

The problem is most of us get tricked out of starting small. Right out of the gates, we start with the wrong mentally. We assume because the dream is big that we need to take big leaps to get there. The truth is the bigger the dream, sometimes the smaller the start. God reveals just enough to get you going. Then, when you're faithful with that, he reveals the next step.

The challenge with small instructions is that they seem insignificant and inconsequential. Yet within those insignificant steps are the very seeds of your success. All throughout the Bible you can read examples of men and women who did amazing feats simple by being faithful to small instructions.

Naaman was told to dip in the Jordan River seven times and was healed of leprosy.

The Israelites were told to walk around Jericho's walls once daily and seven times on the seventh day and the walls fell down flat, and they conquered the city.

Peter, after fishing for hours and catching nothing, was told by Jesus to cast his net on the other side of the boat and received his largest catch of fish.

The disciples were told to hand out the five loaves and two fish that Jesus had prayed for and were able to feed 5,000 men plus women and children.

Noah was instructed to build an ark. Board by board and day-by-day he built. The project took 120 years, but his obedience saved his family of eight while the rest of the human population drowned in a flood.

Know this: your small acts of obedience are never insignificant to God. He will always honor you doing what you can, where you are, with what you have to accomplish his big dream for your life.

So how do we dream big but follow small? Here are some secrets that will help you accomplish God-sized dreams bit-by-bit and day-by-day with less stress and much more success.

- **Start with doing the next indicated thing.** What is that one small thing you know to do that will get you moving in the right direction? Don't overlook the obvious. Life is sending you cues and clues to guide you all the time. Do the next thing you know to do, and then the next indicated thing after that will show up.

> God does not steer a parked car, but he does give directions; stop, go, turn, wait, listen. Follow directions.
> –Greg Moore

- **Narrow your goals.** Better to focus on fewer goals and make more progress than spread yourself too thin. A laser beam gets its power from its precision. When you channel your focus, you supercharge your energy, so aim small.

- **Chunk your big goals down into small bite-sized action steps.** The smaller and more detailed you can make your action steps, the more actionable and immediate they become. If your goal is to lose 30 pounds, chunk it down into action steps like this:

*Goal: Lose 30 pounds in 6 months*

↓

*Lose 5 pounds this month.*

↓

*Lose 1.25 pounds this week.*

↓

*Work out 3 times this week.*

↓

*Go for a 20 minute run Monday/Wednesday/Friday.*

↓

*Go to bed early so I can get up and workout.*

Break your dream down into small action steps and back plan what you can do right now! The smaller and more immediate your action steps are, the better your progress will be. After all, small movements steer great destinies!

- **Intentionally make the bar low.** Set a goal or task to accomplish that almost seems "too easy." Make it so easy that you know without a shadow of a doubt that you can accomplish it. The lower you can make the bar, the easier it will be to overcome your own internal resistance.

- **Choose progress over perfection.** The lie of perfectionism whispers that if you can't do something 100% and do it perfectly, then don't do it at all. Instead, choose to make imperfect progress. If you can't score a touchdown, score a field goal. If you can't workout for an hour, workout for 15 minutes. One imperfect draft of a dissertation beats a perfect thesis idea not begun. Slow progress beats no progress every time!

- **Choose direction over speed.** Don't worry about how long it will take to achieve your dreams or how fast someone else is going. Heading in the right direction is more important than how fast you get there. Life is not a race measured in sprints and splits. It's measured by how well you fulfill what you were called to do. Steer well and stay the course and you'll accomplish all God intended.

> Direction is more important than speed. It doesn't matter how fast you're going if you are headed off a cliff.
> -Darren Hardy

- **Make winning a habit.** When you accomplish an action step, that's called a win. When you repeat the action the next day and then the next, you create a habit of winning! Winning is a habit and so is losing—choose winning.

- **Fail small and start again.** Part of the beauty of taking small steps is the opportunity to make mistakes, learn from them and course correct quickly. So if you try something that doesn't work or if you fall off the wagon all together, just climb back on with the next small step.

## Sweet Life Secrets

- Small acts of obedience are never insignificant to God. He will always honor you doing what you can, where you are, with what you have to accomplish his big dream for your life.

- Life is always sending you clues and cues to guide you towards your destiny. Focus on doing the next indicated thing.

- Take your big dream and chunk it down. The smaller the action steps, the more actionable and immediate they become.

- Choose progress over perfection. Slow progress is better than no progress.

- Celebrate every little success you make along the way. It will keep you motivated to do more.

⬡ 3

# Create a
# Hive of Activity

*The activity you're most avoiding
contains your biggest opportunity.*
*–Robin Sharma*

⬡ BEE
FACT

Inside a single colony are 20,000 to 80,000
worker bees busy with the activities of the hive—
everything from foraging for pollen and nectar, feeding larvae,
fanning their wings to keep the nest cool and defending the
hive among other tasks.

W hen the title and idea for this book first came to my mind, I was thrilled, inspired, and passionate. I couldn't help but imagine all the people who would be impacted by it. I could easily visualize the eye-catching cover of the book and visualize the letters, posts, and emails that I would receive from people whose life had changed thanks to this book. Two years later, only the title was completed, and the shiny luster of the dream had faded to a dull glow. What once seemed like an exhilarating adventure now loomed like a huge mountain— daunting, intimidating, and overwhelming. The more I wanted the goal, the larger the goal seemed to grow until it appeared larger than life.

Eventually I came up with a subtitle and even a table of contents, but every step forward seemed like an excruciating, painstaking effort followed by a longer period of stagnation. I spent days researching and journaling notes without turning any of it into real content. I just couldn't create any momentum.

More than once, I declared, "This weekend I'm going to do nothing but write!" But then the weekend would come and go without any progress. A cycle of inaction began to solidify in my life until one day I realized that if I was going to accomplish this dream, it would take more than simple lip service and random writing attempts. It was going to take me leaning into God's grace, despite the resistance, and completing what He had empowered me to do.

That unshakable intention became unstoppable action. I began waking up at 5 a.m. every morning to write for several hours before starting my day. Soon my daily progress became a rock-solid habit. Today, you hold the result in your hands.

This book was more than a goal; it was the first domino that needed to fall for my dreams to come to pass. That's why I faced such resistance every time I attempted it. On the other side of the completed book was all the other parts of the dream—the website, the vlog, speaking opportunities, and more—that I wanted to pursue in order to motivate and inspire women.

Have you ever felt that way—that there was one thing holding everything else back? That behind just one obstacle waits the life of your dreams?

Enough is enough! It's time to become unstoppable and create a hive of activity.

## Stirring Up the Hive

Creating a hive of activity starts with believing that you are more than a conqueror and called to live the dream God placed on the inside of you. Then, you need to become committed to deliberate action based on that truth.

No matter how big your dream or what you might be lacking in education, talent, or resources—small, intentional steps of action will conquer it every time. Action accelerates direction, aligns circumstances, overcomes obstacles, and attracts opportunities like a magnet. Action is the surest mechanism to defeat fears, self-doubts, and resistance. Dream fulfillment is in the doing!

Whether you've been stuck in a rut, lost your motivation for living your dreams, ignored your endless promises to get started, or allowed your promise to make a change to fall on your own deaf ears, be encouraged. Even if the last sighting of progress was a decade ago, you can create a hive of activity today that will break you through! If you've been striving for your dreams, but you haven't been able to rally your resolve beyond half-hearted efforts, ask God for His grace to finish what He started in you. Receive His grace in faith and resolve to take daily action forward.

Here are the barrier-breaking productivity secrets that God directed me to take along the way that will help you create a hive of activity and accomplish your dreams too:

- **Fill Up to Flow.** A dry well can't pump water. To get a flow of momentum in your life, you must fill up on what fuels your motivation and faith. Talk to others who have achieved what you want. Listen to inspiring podcasts. Read motivational books in the subject area of your dream. Get so full of the Word of God and knowledge about your passion that it can't help but spill out of you into dream action.
- **Visualize Your Victory.** Get a picture of what completion looks like for you. To complete my book, I created a

storyboard of pictures, words, and phrases depicting my book as completed. I included images announcing my book tour, added phrases like "New York Times Best-Selling Author" and pictures of designs I wanted to use in my book and on the cover. Create your own storyboard of success. If you want to lose weight, post pictures of strong, lean bodies. Even glue your face on them to make it more concrete. If you want a happier, healthier marriage, post pictures of smiling couples in love, and words that speak to it. If you can see it, you can be it.

- **Fix Your Focus.** Because your dream achievement has to happen as part of your everyday life that doesn't mean you get to ditch your everyday responsibilities of work, home, and family life to go on a dream hiatus—but you can decide to make dream achievement your focus and eliminate all other distractions. Make a list of the things that distract you from taking action on your dreams, and eliminate or minimize them.

- **Trade Up.** For a season, decide that you will trade up and dedicate all discretionary time for dream action. Trade up your TV time after work for an hour or two of working on your dream. Trade up that extra hour of sleep in the morning to tackle your next action step. Trade up mindless time on social media for reading a book or building your brand. When you fix your focus and rally your available resources, you will make significant progress.

- **Get in Motion.** It's a scientific law that an object in motion tends to stay in motion while an object at rest tends to stay at rest. When you get home from work, stay in motion. Instead of vegging out in front of the TV, think of one action you can take each day to move closer to your dream.

- **Make an Action List.** Create a dream action plan. List all the steps you can take toward your dream in the next 24 hours—even if it's just one. Next, make a list of all the steps you can complete in the 7 days. Make each of these action steps easily doable to motivate you to build on your success. Then, make a list of all the steps you can complete in the next month. Finally make a list of action steps to complete in the next 6 months. With your lists in hand, go for it. Start today.

You were created to live a life of dream achievement! Create a hive of activity and watch the Sweet Life that flows from your newfound focus.

## Sweet Life Secrets

- Unshakable intention creates unstoppable action.

- Dream fulfillment is in the doing.

- Action is the surest mechanism to defeat fears, self-doubts, and resistance.

- Ask God for His grace to finish what He started in you.

- Read through the barrier-breaking productivity secrets in the preceding pages. Which one do you need to put into action next? Resolve to get started with that habit today.

⟨ 4 ⟩

# Experience the Wonder

*Wisdom begins in wonder.*
*–Socrates*

I remember it clear as day. Our pajama-clad figures were whisked out of bed and into the car in the wee hours of the night for our adventure into the countryside. As the city lights faded farther and farther behind us, the night sky grew dark, black, and peaceful.

We arrived at our destination—a cozy field far out in the middle of nowhere—and the seven of us, my parents and siblings, used flashlights to spread quilts and blankets onto the lush meadow grass. The dew-covered grass smelled sweet as we lay on our backs staring up into the star-strewn heavens. We were millions of miles away, yet felt like we could touch the stars with our fingertips.

With anticipation we held our breath as my mom whispered the words, "Just wait for it..." Moments later, the heavens exploded. Shooting stars zipped and whizzed across the nighttime sky as the meteor shower began. What a breathtaking sight! It was our own personal fireworks show with all the glory of the heavens on display. Staring into the sky, I felt small yet connected to something great, vast, and mysterious. Even today, this childhood memory is so vivid it only takes closing my eyes to transport me back to that momentum of breathtaking wonder.

Merriam Webster defines wonder as "a cause of astonishment or admiration, marvel or miracle." Moments of wonder can appear in our lives out of nowhere. They are the moments when we feel most alive, joyous, and grateful to be a part of the miracle of it all. They instill in us a bit of awe, majesty, and humility and make us feel a part of something bigger than ourselves. For some, it's watching the setting sun as brilliant streaks of red, purple, and blue saturate the horizon. For others, it's capturing the sweet expression on a sleeping child's face. Wonder can even be witnessing an Olympic athlete who leans in to win the gold by a thousandth of a second. These incredible feats are the moments that take our breath away, stir our passion, or cause us to hunger for something more in our own lives.

I would rather have a mind opened by wonder than one closed by belief.
–Gerry Spence

Don't lose the wonder. Moments like these are necessary to the Sweet Life.

## The Wonder Quest

As I've been on my own wonder quest, I want to share with you some secrets I've found to experience more of it in your life:

**Open your eyes to see your life and world anew.** When was the last time you were moved, mesmerized, fascinated, or flabbergasted? Recapture childlike amazement. Don't be so burdened down with your daily responsibilities or bored by your routine that you miss the infinite invitations to experience the wonder that each day presents. Actively look for moments in your day that make you feel alive, joyful, or reflective. There's something there waiting to be discovered. Gretchen Rueben said it best, "The days are long, but the years are short." There's majesty to be had in the moments, my sweet friend.

> It is a happiness to wonder—it is a happiness to dream.
> -Edgar Allan Poe

**Create a wonder list.** Your life tells a story—the story of you. It's a story of what makes you happy, what makes you laugh, and what intrigues you. Pay attention. What are the moments that make your soul come alive? Write them down. This is your wonder list. And a funny thing happens: as you celebrate and appreciate these moments, more of them seem to appear.

**Be open to wonder wherever you may find it.** Sometimes wonder is so random it can catch you by surprise. It's the loving glance from your spouse that makes you blush. It's opening the mail to find a surprise care package from a far-away friend. The moment needn't be big or extravagant to hold a bit of magic. It merely needs to be noticed and appreciated.

**Expect God to do wonderful things in your life.** You are a wonder. There has never been nor will ever be anyone like

# My Wonder List

This is what takes my breath away: _____

_____

_____

These are the things that make me feel alive: _____

_____

_____

These are the things that capture my curiosity:_____

_____

_____

These are the things that make me feel connected to miracles: _____

_____

_____

## HERE ARE SOME THINGS ON MY WONDER LIST:

- The sweet smile on my newborn son's face as he sleeps
- My husband's untiring devotion to daily better our marriage and family
- Quiet moments of solitude sipping a good cup of coffee
- Long nature walks listening to chatty birds and gurgling brooks
- The smell just before it rains
- The intrigue of a good book
- The amazing friends and family that I get to do life with

you on this planet. You are a miracle, and you were created as part of a perfect plan that is infinitely bigger than any of us. Live each day believing that God has great things in store for you. Expect God to do the miraculous and the marvelous in your life to fulfill the purpose He created you for.

**Find wonder in your journey.** What if rather than looking for mountain-top moments we learned to find beauty in the journey? Then every day—valley or peak—we could find a bit of something to learn from. When you are grateful and appreciate the beauty of where you are, you are positioned to embrace the future.

The Sweet Life is a wonder-filled life that you get to pursue day after day. Always seek the wonder. To this day, I still look up into the evening sky hoping to catch a glimpse of a shooting star.

## Sweet Life Secrets

- Actively look for moments in your day that make you feel alive, joyful, or even reflective.

- Expect God to do the miraculous and the marvelous in your life to fulfill the purpose He created you for.

- Find beauty in your journey and learn to be grateful for where you are.

- Create your wonder list using the prompts on the previous page.

# ⟨5⟩

# Banish the Buzz

*Almost everything will work again if you unplug it for a*
*few minutes, including you.*
*–Anne Lamott*

**BEE FACT**

The honeybee's wings stroke incredible fast, about 200 beats per second, thus making their famous, distinctive buzz.

I have a confession to make. I am distracted more than I'd like. It's not always easy for me to disconnect. I love online research, playing Words with Friends, and listening to my favorite podcast. While the buzz recharges me in excited doses, too much of it leaves me depleted.

I've been sucked into television or social media, procrastinating instead of working on things that need to get done. I'll even admit that I feel relatively naked when I'm without my cell phone. It's true…I've become bound to "the buzz" in ways that are not always in my best interest, or even the most satisfying—and they're far from conducive to the Sweet Life.

One thing is certain—the buzz is everywhere! We live in a media-saturated, tech-charged world where digital distraction is the norm. Information is more accessible, and devices more portable than ever.

Modern technology informs us and educates us, but it also means that we're constantly bombarded by political pundits, the threat of economic catastrophe, and terrorist attacks, not to mention the 24/7 windows we have into others' lives (or at least to their highlight reel!). All this access can make life distorted and skewed towards fear, comparison, and information overload.

In a world that's more connected than ever, we can also become more disconnected from each other. We've all seen the couple sitting in a restaurant dining together but texting rather than talking. Or how about the group of friends hanging out but with everyone zoned in on their phones? I'll be the first to raise my hand and say that I'm guilty of texting my husband sitting in the next room because I didn't feel like getting up and walking 10 feet to tell him something. Modern technology can be convenient, but used excessively, it can be alienating.

Turn off your email; turn off your phone; disconnect from the Internet; figure out a way to set limits so you can concentrate when you need to, and disengage when you need to. Technology is a good servant but a bad master.
–Gretchen Rubin

Rest assured: I'm not here to bash technology. It has many amazing benefits and plays an important role in making our world more global. It makes our lives easier and more efficient. But I am advocating for not letting technology and access to information consume you to the point where you are never alone with your own thoughts, or to where you forget the importance of having down time to tune in to yourself and to those around you.

## Heart to Heart

The Sweet Life is found when you become intentional

about carving out time for personal reflection and genuine connection with others. The needs of others and the cry for community cannot be met screen to screen; it must be met face to face and heart to heart.

When you banish the buzz, you can hear the Holy Spirit and His words of direction and protection for your life.

When you banish the buzz, you can recharge, refocus, and find creative solutions to problems that you're facing.

When you banish the buzz, you can gain perspective, gather strength, and sharpen your focus.

When you banish the buzz, you can see the needs of others, hear their cry for community, and step in to connect and comfort.

I recently had a friend who quit his six-figure job. His family knew it was time to unplug and start "living memorably" as they traveled the United States and experienced nature. They sold their home, bought an RV, and took the plunge. Before setting off for their adventure, one of the big things they wrestled with was how much technology to take. Both he and his wife were freelance writers, so they needed

We've become so focused on that tiny screen that we forget the big picture, the people right in front of us.
–Regina Brett

to have access to computers and Wi-Fi to stay employed on the road. And with their three children being teens and preteens, they certainly didn't want to outlaw gaming consoles, phones, iPads, and television completely lest they face a full-scale mutiny... yet they wanted their children to see and experience something different. Part of the point of it all was to disconnect from the virtual world and experience the breathtaking real world. In the end, they decided to limit tech time to just a small portion of their day and maximize the adventure. From Mt. Rushmore to Yellowstone Park to lesser-known sites like Billy the Kid's grave, they bonded like never before and gained a deeper appreciation for the world and one another.

Making your year memorable by being intentional. You might be someone who prefers stillness, or you might feed off the frenzy. Regardless of where you fall on that pendulum, it's necessary to manage the amount of buzz you allow in your life. Here are some tips that have helped me set boundaries for the buzz, and I believe they will help you too.

## Buzz Killers: How to Set Boundaries on the Buzz

- **Have a cut off time.** Set a time after which you won't read email, skim social media, surf the web, text, or game.
- **Be present in the moment.** Whether traveling for vacation, enjoying a birthday party, or going for a walk, breathe in the experience instead of scrambling to snap, tweet, text, or live stream it. Simply be present. Relish what you are doing in the moment and enjoy who you are with rather than rushing to share it with the world.
- **Seek out genuine human contact and community.** Take your relationships offline and pursue in-person contact rather than virtual. Connection and intimacy are birthed in community, so seek the company of others. Find a church small group to join, attend a live networking event, or meet up with a friend for coffee.
- **Streamline your digital diet.** Gate yourself and make sure the information that gets to you is worth your time and attention. Set up filters and organize your social media

accounts. Dial down your notifications. Unsubscribe from unnecessary emails and declutter your inbox.

- **Follow through with face time.** Never use digital communication to avoid having face-to-face conversations. If you find yourself wanting to hide behind an email, text, or social comment, resist the urge and go seek out the person you need to communicate with instead. There's so much that can be misunderstood through a digital sound bite, but understanding and connection come from intentional face-to-face communication.

- **Designate tech-free time.** Protect your hours of peak productivity from tech time wasters. Carve out an hour or two each day to tackle your biggest project or engage in a hobby without digital distraction. If you really need to focus, choose one day a week for a tech-Sabbath and enjoy a whole day unplugged.

- **Choose your channel.** Limit the ways you digest information to just a few choice channels. It may be from a favorite podcast, blogger, social influencer, news broadcast, or television show. Be selective and choose specific content to inspire and inform you in manageable doses.

## Sweet Life Secrets

- Carve out time for personal reflection and genuine connection with others.

- Take your relationships offline and pursue in-person contact over virtual.

- Gate yourself and make sure the information that gets to you is worth your time and attention.

- Protect your hours of peak productivity from tech time wasters.

- Be selective and choose specific content to inspire and inform you in manageable doses.

# Don't Overthink or You Will Sink

*Thoughts are like an open ocean, they can either move you forward within its waves, or sink you under deep into its abyss.*
*—Anthony Liccione*

W hat is one of the nosiest, busiest places on Earth? A school playground at recess? A stadium before a big game? A beehive buzzing with thousands of bees? No…it's *your mind*! I'll be the first to admit my thoughts can race faster than a sports car on the German Autobahn and be louder than a sold-out rock concert. One thing is certain; it's hard to live the Sweet Life with a frenzied mind.

Ever had a day where your mind spun round and round like a record player stuck on the same mental track? Yup, me too! The brain is an amazing creation. When you think, neurons fire along a neural pathway in your brain. Every time you think the same thought, the faster the neurons fire on that path. The brain likes shortcuts, so it doesn't have to work as hard. The more you think the thought, the easier it is for the brain to do it again. Obsessive thoughts are empowered through this repetition. If you're thinking about the right things, then you'll have more right thoughts. But if you're thinking about the wrong things, then you empower a negative thought cycle.

Mental misery can come in many forms—racing, intrusive thoughts, repetitive mental loops, addictive worry, habitual fretting, and even obsessive-compulsive anxiety disorder. Overthinking by any name spells misery. Two of the most common ways to get mentally stuck are through *rumination* and *worry*.

- *Rumination* is when you obsess over past events—often replaying them again and again in your mind.
- *Worry* is when you obsess over future events and imagine scenario after scenario of what-ifs.

At the core of obsessive thoughts is conditioned thinking rooted in fear, low expectations, and outdated beliefs. The French once called obsessive compulsive disorder *folie de doute,* translated "the doubting disease." That's what obsessive thoughts are—your doubts on constant repeat.

God gave us our minds to think, but not to overthink. When we think too long about a situation, we reveal a lack of trust in God and get ourselves into trouble. The Bible says fretting—which is a constant state of worry or anxiety—only leads to evil (Psalm 37:8). We can ruminate on a situation so much that we worry ourselves into a bad decision. When we overthink, we sink!

Your mind has a spin cycle to it. You can either spin up thoughts of life, peace, hope, possibilities, and success, or you can spin up thoughts of fear, lack, worry, doubt, and failure. The

Bible tells us in Philippians 4:8 what we should focus our minds on. Think on things that are:

True
Honorable
Worthy of respect
Right and just
Pure and wholesome
Lovely
Admirable and commendable
Excellent
Worthy of praise

Take mental inventory. Do your thoughts align with this list? If not, it's time to stop and swap thoughts!

## Your Thoughts, Your Choice

Now for the good news...You get to choose what you think! You don't have to stay stuck in mental misery. You can master your mind and control your thoughts rather than letting them control you. When you make your mind your ally rather than your enemy, you can live in confidence, think thoughts of life and peace, and win over worry. Here are some powerful techniques I've discovered over the years to take charge of my mind and stop obsessing. They can work for you too:

**Name it and Tame It.** Identify the thought. What is it you fear or doubt? Name it. For example, "I'm afraid of running this business on my own for fear I'm going to fail." When you define what is at the root of your intrusive thoughts, you begin to dilute its power over your mind. Clarity will position you to deal with the fear through proactive action steps.

**Put it on Pause.** When incessant worry pops up, schedule a reflection time for you to think over what you're obsessing about. Carve out 15 minutes in the evening when you can mull the intrusive thought over, but until then, when it pops up, tell yourself, "Sorry, this is not the time for that. I'll circle back to you at 7 p.m. and then you can have 15 minutes to reflect until your heart's content."

**Make Decisions Decisively.** Most decisions are the baker's dozen of daily life—they are relatively unimportant and can be made quickly. Should I eat this or that? Go here or there? Should I make lasagna or baked chicken for dinner? These are many of the things we overthink, distracting ourselves from using our time and mental energy more wisely. I know I've pondered what to do for dinner before and rather than make a quick decision, I started flipping through recipes—which led me to read articles on which foods are healthy and which were not—which led me to research a new scale to buy for myself—which led me to Google cute workout clothes—which led me to Pinterest—where I totally got distracted looking at things completely unrelated to food. Needless to say, two hours later, I was no closer to deciding what to make for dinner and I wasted a bunch of time. Make daily decisions quickly and don't overthink them. Usually, one outcome or choice is as good as the next.

**Get a Partner and Get Perspective.** Sometimes we are so in our own heads with an obsessive mental loop that we need a friend to bounce our thoughts off of and pull us back from the brink. Often after I've shared with a trusted girlfriend what I'm obsessing over, she can point out my exaggerated thinking and sift through facts, fears, and fantasies. In the end, we can laugh at how far off in Crazyland my thoughts had taken me.

**List the Lesson.** Turn your obsessive thought into a lesson learned. Instead of replaying an incessant loop where you made a mistake or failed, pull out a pen and write down what lesson you learned in the situation. Describe it in one sentence or less. Then be done with it, knowing you learned from it and are moving forward as a stronger, wise, and better person for the experience.

I once had a boss take me to task in front of my team over expectations he had not communicated to me. My reaction was to stand up for myself, defend myself, and explain that I was happy to execute them going forward, but these expectations had not been communicated before. While I was proud of myself for what I said, I began to obsess over how I said it. My voice had been shaky, and I was emotional and felt flustered. My obsessive thoughts kept replaying the scene again and again— of course with a spotlight on me and how uncomposed and attacked I felt. To end this painful replay, here's the one sentence lesson I wrote down in my journal: When I feel attacked, I will take a minute to gather my thoughts and composure, and then communicate in a calm, confident manner. Lesson learned and case closed!

**Get Physical.** Oftentimes when we overthink, we live in the past or in the future. To get out of your head and ground yourself in the present moment, get physical. Go for a walk, exercise, or take a few minutes to stretch. Focus on your physical senses and observe the noises and sights that surround you. Self-soothe by doing something artistic like drawing or dancing. Even simply rubbing your earlobes can release positive endorphins and snap you back to the present.

**Forgive Yourself and Let It Go.** Learn to accept yourself—imperfections and all—rather than obsess incessantly on your faults, flaws, and mistakes. When I've questioned my decisions or feel I've made a mistake, I've had to forgive myself and move on. Perfection is not required for a purpose-filled, joyful life. Look at your scars, setbacks, and sorrows as a work of beauty that helped you become the stronger, wiser person you are today and use these experiences to encourage others.

What are you replaying in your mind? Is there something you just can't quite understand—a loss, a betrayal, or a disappointment? Is there a failure that you keep replaying in your mind, holding your own feet to the fire and blaming yourself for the outcome? Learn to mentally accept things as they are and LET IT GO!

As you let go of the obsessive thoughts, you'll lay hold of the Sweet Life, I promise!

## Sweet Life Secrets

- Your thoughts are strengthened through repetition. If you think about the right things, then you'll have more right thoughts.

- Focus your mind on things that are true, honorable, worthy of respect, right, pure, wholesome, admirable, peaceful, lovely, excellent, and praiseworthy.

- Choose what you think! You don't have to stay stuck in mental misery.

- Define what is at the root of your intrusive thoughts by giving it a name, and you will dilute its power over your mind.

- Learn to accept yourself—imperfections and all—rather than obsess incessantly on your faults, flaws, and mistakes.

# 7

# Girlfriends and Good Times are Necessary

*Friendship between women is different than friendship between men. We talk about different things. We delve deep. We go under, even if we haven't seen each other for years ... It's my women friends that keep starch in my spine and without them, I don't know where I would be.*
*–Jane Fonda, Vanity Fair, January 2015*

**BEE FACT**

Bees Friend is the name of a beautiful purple or blue flower that attracts pollinators like bees and other insects. It is considered one of the top 20 honey-producing flowers.

D riving to Cracker Barrel to meet my friend Jennifer for breakfast, I was reflecting on all the things I had to share with her, and this chapter title came to mind. It was at a pivotal time in my life, and I had decided to switch jobs. I was leaving a job that allowed me to work from home in my pajamas with flexible hours—and I was moving to a job with a 45-minute commute, but greater opportunity to explore my gifts and talents, and be challenged in new ways.

At the time, my husband and I were trying to get pregnant with our first child, and my friend Jennifer was a few months into her pregnancy. She and her husband were facing many of the same decisions we were. Decisions about:

maternity benefits
planning for a family
upgrading to a family SUV
whether to be working moms or career moms or both
how to balance marriage, motherhood, ministry, serving, and personal time
whether to continue leading an area of ministry or focus on the private pursuits God had given us
how to encourage our husbands in their calling
intimate questions about marriage, aging gracefully, and more

It's good to be a woman; we're gifted at covering this many topics in two hours!

Over pancakes and scrambled eggs, we were able to unscramble the questions in our hearts, share our hopes and dreams, and pray for each other before heading home. I left with a full belly and an even fuller heart. My soul's cup was truly running over… and the several cups of java I had downed were delicious too.

He who walks with the wise grows wise, but a companion of fools suffers harm.
–Proverb 13:20

My friendships are my treasure. Whether near or far, God has always surrounded me with gal pals rich in love, character, wisdom, and fun. We've danced and celebrated on the heights of joy together and walked arm in arm through dark valleys and tough places.

In fact, the night before my previously mentioned breakfast outing, Andrea—another dear friend of mine in Oregon whose friendship dates back to high school—had just encouraged me with these words in a text message:

*"God provides people in our lives we call friends to accompany us and help us bear one another's burdens as we face the complexities of life."*

It's true; girlfriends make life sweet!

Girlfriends confirm the dreams in our heart.

Girlfriends reassure us and help us overcome our insecurities.

Girlfriends listen and offer wise counsel.

Girlfriends hear what's not being said.

Girlfriends help steer us away from unsafe paths.

Girlfriends sharpen us and encourage us to reach our true potential.

Girlfriends share truth without tearing us down.

Girlfriends multiply our joys and divide our sorrows.

All of these things are true if you have the *right* girlfriends. Seek to surround yourself with encouragers, vision pursuers, and dream builders. Rethink gal pals whose idea of friendship is belittling comments, grudging compliments, or brash behavior.

No person is your friend who demands your silence, or denies your right to grow.
–Alice Walker

Know this—your Sweet Life peeps are out there. They are! Those who love to live big and laugh loud. Those who get you and understand you. Those who celebrate your unique glitter and shine because they reflect the same style of joyful living. Release those with half-hearted hurrahs and lukewarm welcomes. Embrace the certainty that your true friends are Heaven-assigned and will show up in life along the path you're traveling. As you're looking for them, they are looking for you! And remember, the best way to attract a Sweet Life friend is to be one to someone else.

# Seven of the Greatest Girlfriends in History

## 1    Mercy Otis Warren and Abigail Adams

Friends for almost a half of century, these two women were bold, passionate and highly educated revolutionaries. Abigail Adams, wife of Founding Father John Adams, was a passionate advocate for women's rights and is most known for a March 1776 letter to her husband reminding him to "remember the ladies" when passing laws and policy. Mercy Otis Warren was the spouse of John Warren, a political writer of the Revolution, and a champion for equality between men and women. Ahead of their time, these women forged a friendship through years of correspondence leaving a literary legacy in their quest for freedom and change.

## 2    George Eliot and Harriet Beecher Stowe

American author of Uncle Tom's Cabin, Harriet Beecher Stowe, and English novelist George Elliot were close friends until death. Never having met in person, these two legendary authors became transatlantic pen pals writing letters to each other for 11 years. Despite being on opposite sides of the ocean, they consistently supported one another and shared advice on writing, women's suffrage, family, and more.

## 3    The Edinburgh Seven

This group of women were pals who fought to become the first women to go to medical school in the United

Kingdom. They began studying medicine at the University of Edinburgh in 1869, but in the end, they were barred from graduating and becoming doctors. While disappointing, their determination to push back against sexist rules gained national attention, and eventually put women's rights on the national agenda. This led to laws in 1876 that allowed women to study medicine at university, paving the way for generations of female doctors.

## Lucille Ball and Vivian Vance          4

"I Love Lucy" stars Lucille Ball and Ethel Mertz weren't just co-stars but tight-knit friends. In a day when female comedians were rare, the two excelled at comedic chemistry and timing. Vance one said, "We fought like sisters and made up like sisters. We adored each other's company." They not only pushed each other to be funnier, but also supported each other through painful situations. Vance had an abusive husband who mistreated her emotionally and physically, and Ball eventually convinced her friend to leave him. The two were the best of friends to the end of their lives.

## Marilyn Monroe and Ella Fitzgerald          5

Iconic Ella Fitzgerald attributes her big break to an unlikely figure—Marilyn Monroe. Apparently, when the 20-time-Grammy nominated singer tried to book a gig at the Mocambo in Hollywood in 1955, the manager turned her away because of the color of her skin. Monroe thought this ridiculous and said that she would sit front row every night if Fitzgerald got the job, promising to pull in not only massive crowds, but the press. "I owe Marilyn Monroe a real debt," Fitzgerald would say later. "After that I never had to play a small jazz club again. She was an unusual woman—and ahead of her time, and she didn't know it."

## 6    Oprah Winfrey and Gayle King

These two powerful women in media share one of the most iconic and enduring friendships. The pair met in 1976 while working at a Baltimore television station—Gayle was production assistant at the time and Oprah was the evening news anchor. Over the next four decades, Gayle and Oprah were never far apart. Gayle served as editor in chief of *O Magazine* and special correspondent on The Oprah Winfrey Show and eventually landed in her own starring role as anchor of CBS This Morning. In a special tribute article about their 40+ year friendship, Oprah had this to say about King: "And no matter how many ventures or adventures we undertake—whatever life has to offer— we'll be in each other's corner. Solid. Timeless. Forever."

## 7    Tina Fey and Amy Poehler

These two queens of comedy have been close friends for decades. Since meeting in 1993 at an improv comedy class the two have had wildly successful and often intersecting careers that included Saturday Night Live sketches to hosting the Golden Globes together. When Poehler finally joined SNL, Fey recorded in her memoir Bossypants, "I was so happy. Weirdly, I remember thinking, 'My friend is here! My friend is here!' Even though things had been going great for me at the show, with Amy there, I felt less alone."

## Friendship Is as Friendship Does

Friendship is give and take, ebb and flow, so always invest richly in your friendships. There will be times when you need to lean a little more on your friends and pull from the coffers of care, so be sure you are also being intentional to make regular deposits of love, concern, celebration, and support into your friends' lives. Do the things that make them feel loved and be the kind of friend you expect. We all get busy, but it's important to keep your friendships in good repair.

> A friend is one that knows you as you are, understands where you have been, accepts what you have become, and still, gently allows you to grow.
> –William Shakespeare

I have a group of three friends whose friendship spans the past 25 years. Since we're all super busy, in different seasons of life, and live in different states, the easiest way for us to stay connected is through a group text. We regularly text pictures of family, random memes, tidbits about our day and lives, and even share concerns and advice. Although phone calls are rare, our hearts stay knit across the miles.

Find what works best to stay close to your friends. Whether you catch up with phone calls, send snail mail, plan girl's nights, or share Pinterest boards to plan birthday parties for the kids, make sure you take time to connect with and engage your friends and their worlds.

It takes effort to keep friendships fresh. Don't let your Sweet Life relationships grow stale or routine. Mix things up and try new things together. Travel to a new part of the world as a group or tackle a new hobby. Adventures are the memory makers of our lives.

While some friends are only for a season in life, true friendships don't have expiration dates. Lifelong friendships feel like your favorite oversized sweater—familiar, cozy and comfy with plenty of room to grow. Friendships age through the years, but the best ones never go out of style.

## Sweet Life Secrets

- Show up for your friends when it matters. Schedule regular girlfriend time, whether weekly, monthly, or quarterly.

- Have fun with your friends. Go to the spa, the gym, or a flea market. Enjoy a movie marathon, concert in the park, or cooking together. Plan a girlfriend getaway or vacation. Whatever you enjoy doing together, silliness, shenanigans, giggles, and goofs are always encouraged.

- Think about thoughtful things you can do for your friends that don't require a lot of time or money. Text a compliment or a prayer. Celebrate your friendversary by posting your favorite picture of the two of you together and tell her why you treasure her friendship.

- Be genuine with your friendships. Accept your friends for who they are and allow them to know the real you, not a phony facade.

- Treasure old friends but make room for new ones.

# 8

# Cut the Comparison

*We struggle with insecurity because we compare our behind-the-scenes with everyone else's highlight reel.*
*–Steven Furtick*

**BEE FACT**

Bees and wasps look similar, but comparatively they are very different. Bees have hairy body and legs, are pollinators and less aggressive, and live in geometric wax hives. Wasps, on the other hand, have smooth body and legs, are predators and typically more aggressive, and live in papery nests.

L et's be honest: in the social media era, it's easy to compare. For me, however, comparison was a trap the enemy laid long before social media existed. In college, I struggled horribly with comparison. I have a bold, direct, get-to-the-bottom-line personality, and I would always compare myself to my friends who were sweet, poised, and reserved. In my mind, everyone liked them, and so I wanted to be soft spoken and meek like them, too. But try as I might, no matter how I attempted to reign in my outgoing, outspoken personality, my take-charge, speak-out boldness came to the surface. What I didn't understand at the time was that the seed of confidence and courage within me was my *uniqueness*; it wasn't a weakness. It was part of my

God-given identity. Comparison will always do that—take your uniqueness and turn it into a weakness by comparing it to someone else's strength.

After years of downplaying and devaluing my personality, I decided to embrace who God created me to be. As I asked God to reveal my uniqueness, I discovered that along with my boldness came a fun-loving, adventurous, truth-speaking personality that has a passion for helping other women live their dreams, find fulfillment, and make a difference. I am uniquely created the way I am because of who I'm called to help. Now I confidently embrace my uniqueness, and I help others fight to do the same.

Sweet friends, let's be real: it can be a battle sometimes. And the battle doesn't stop with your identity. Comparison only starts with attacking your identity. Next, it will often expand into your outlook on life—if you let it.

I have found this truth to be ironic but true: my appreciation for what I have is in direct proportion to what I compare it to. When I see someone going through a hard time or a loss, I am forever grateful for what I have been given, and my heart is filled with gratitude. Other times, when I look at someone else's seemingly picture-perfect life on social media, someone accomplishing something, I feel like I don't measure up—all because I compared my daily life to someone else's highlight reel.

## The Comparison Game

Here's how silly comparison can be. While driving I often played the comparison game. When stuck in commuter traffic, you must continually determine which lane to drive in. A little assessment and you hope you pick the fast-moving lane. Well, silly me, I took the "I'm moving faster than you are" game to a whole other level.

I would choose the lane I wanted, but if torn between two, I would look at the car next to me and make a mental note of it. *Looks like my neighbor in the blue Honda Civic is about even with me.* Then, I would proceed to track whether I stayed ahead of my neighbor or if I had indeed chosen the slower lane. Hey, we've all been there! We jump in the lane that we think is moving faster only to have it come to a dead standstill while the lane we just left speeds up and flies by.

That's exactly what would happen to me…again and again. I would be stopped and see the Honda Civic I was tracking, pick the right lane and cruise 20 cars ahead of me. I'd get so frustrated my slow pace and progress. *If only I had chosen the other lane! Then I would be where that Honda was now enjoying the speed and freedom of the open lane!*

On the flipside, if my lane was the one that gained distance, then I'd pat myself on the back for choosing correctly and outpacing the Honda. Can you see how maddening and pointless this is? Ha! Comparing ourselves to other drivers is as silly as comparing ourselves to our friends and acquaintances, yet it's easy to be tempted to do this. We turn our focus away from our own lives and on to another person, watching how they run their race and live their life, and we start measuring ourselves by how well we're keeping up and whether we're "getting ahead" of them or "falling behind."

The truth is, we all have our own race to run; it's not a competition. **God did not design your life using the pattern of someone else's.**

For we dare not class ourselves or compare ourselves with those who commend themselves. But they, measuring themselves by themselves, and comparing themselves among themselves, are not wise.

–2 Corinthians 10:12

You have a unique purpose and destiny. The pace for your life is unique to you, and you don't have to measure yourself by others.

Some of us have seasons where we move fast and have open windows of opportunity that we can seize and capitalize on by God's grace. At the same time, we all have seasons where it seems like life stands still, where we're trying to do the best we can. Differing cycles and seasons are a part of life, so don't foolishly compare yourself to others.

The Bible says the race is not given to the swift or to the strong, but time and chance happen to everyone (Ecclesiastes 9:11). God will make sure the right doors open for you when you need them and when you're ready for them. So, don't feel like you're behind or pride yourself that you're ahead. Just run your race and run it to the best of your ability without pridefully comparing yourself to others.

Comparison starts with attacking your identity and will often expand into your outlook if you let it.

At its root, comparison is a lie and a trap. It either creates a cycle of pride or discouragement. It traps you with thoughts like, *My life is so much better than hers!* or *I wish I had her lifestyle…family…husband…looks…influence… accomplishments…waistline…* _____ *[you fill in the blank].*

The list of what the enemy wants us to compare never ends. Sweet friend, I'm going to share some hard truth with you and I want you to get it—way down in your soul: There will *always* be someone to compare yourself to, but don't, because it's a trap!

## The Weapons of Our Warfare

Comparison is a destructive force that will eat at your soul the more you indulge in it. The enemy's goal is to use comparison to rob you of your God-given identity and uniqueness—and cause you to lose sight of the Sweet Life God has planned for you to live. He wants to blind you to who you are and what you already possess.

Thankfully, God hasn't left us defenseless to fend off this fiendish foe. God has given you and me two powerful weapons to wield that have transformative power to cut comparison off at the root and cause you to see it for what it is—a lie. The first weapon is a spirit of thankfulness, and the second is the knowledge of our sufficiency in Christ.

When comparison tries to raise its ugly head, recognize the thought. Then, take up your weapon of thankfulness.

Say aloud, *"No, I'm not going to compare. I choose to be grateful."* Begin to name out loud what you're grateful for. Soon the feelings of angst and despair caused by comparison will subside. Instead, you will be filled with a spirit of praise, gratefulness, peace, and joy.

Then, pack the one-two punch and take it a step further: Acknowledge that you are sufficient in Christ. Understand that you are complete in God and that in Him you possess all you need. You are not lacking, inferior, or deficient. As a child of God, you are created with infinite value and can celebrate the infinite value and worth of others.

We won't be distracted by comparison if we are captivated with purpose.
–Bob Goff

When a comparative thought strikes, you can boldly declare, "I have no need to compare because I am more than enough. God supplies all my needs. I am living my Sweet Life and I can celebrate with others in theirs."

I applied these powerful principals in my life and overcame status anxiety and competitive comparison. Now I approach each day with the attitude that I'm exactly where I'm supposed to be and that I will get to where I need to go at the right time, under the right circumstances, with the right people, according to God's perfect plan.

Don't believe the lie of comparison. Comparison focuses on what's *measurable* and *temporal*. The Sweet Life focuses on what's *eternal* and *infinite*. The likes you get on social media don't last; what lasts is the unshakable, incomparable truth of knowing your contentment and worth is founded in Christ alone.

## Sweet Life Secrets

- Your uniqueness is not a weakness. It is a part of your God-given identity. Cherish it.

- The race and pace for your life is unique to you, and you don't have to measure yourself by others.

- At its root, comparison is a lie and a trap. Choose to break the cycle of pride or discouragement trapping your thought life.

- To battle comparison, take up your weapons of thankfulness and the knowledge of your sufficiency in Christ.

# 9

# Use a Spoonful of Honey

*Be an encourager.*
*The world has plenty of critics already.*
*–Dave Willis*

⬡ **BEE FACT**

Honey has long been regarded as a medicinal aid used in a variety of ways. Since ancient times, raw honey has been used to cure all manner of ills including dressing wounds, reducing scarring, anti-inflammatory uses, and stimulating new tissue growth.

Who doesn't love to be with an encourager? Encouragers are like a breath of fresh air. They breathe life into you, fill you with confidence, and boost your spirits. When you encourage someone, you breathe hope into them. Like honey, encouragement is healing. It sinks into your deepest wounds and scars and has the ability to raise you to a new level, instill hope, and fuel you with fresh energy and vision.

When you make it your goal in life to encourage others, you will find more and more people encouraging you. One of my favorite Bible verses says, "Those who refresh others will themselves be refreshed" (Proverbs 11:25, NLT).

If you are in a place where you feel like you could use some encouragement, then start looking for others to encourage. Speak encouraging words to your spouse. Encourage your children. Encourage your friends. Encourage your coworkers and your boss. Encourage your parents, siblings, and relatives. Encourage your neighbors, pastors, and your kids' teachers. Encourage strangers—someone standing behind you in the checkout line, your waitress, or your favorite Starbucks barista. Believe me, they need it.

The list of people you can encourage is endless. Encourage whoever, however, and whenever and you will reap what you sow—I promise. It's one of the secrets to the Sweet Life.

> Everyone has the potential to be an encourager. You don't have to be rich. You don't have to be a genius. You don't have to have it all together. All you have to do is care about people and initiate.
> –John Maxwell

Right now, think of one person in your world who needs encouragement. Write down their name and one thing you can do or say to encourage them.

My husband is especially great at encouraging young people. He has a natural way with teenagers and young adults and speaks words of life and praise into them even when they're on bad behavior. When he has the opportunity to speak to teens in juvenile detention centers and halfway homes, he tells them:

*"You have worth."*

*"There is greatness in you."*

*"I see you doing something significant in this world."*

Those words of confidence are often the very thing that helps them shift their perspective and make better choices for their future.

We all need an encourager in our lives if we are going to achieve great things. No success is fulfilled alone. Paul was one of the great men of the Bible, writing two-thirds of the New Testament. But he didn't do it alone. One of his closest friends and traveling mates was a lesser-known man named Joseph. The disciples nicknamed him "Barnabus," which means, "son of encouragement." Imagine being such an encourager that your friends nicknamed you, "The Great Encourager!" I'm making that one of my secret goals in life. Seek to be an encourager and seek to surround yourself with encouragers.

## Looking Out for Encouragement

There are so many ways to encourage those around you. You can send an encouraging text, give an encouraging hug, do an encouraging act of service, or surprise someone with an encouraging gift.

My love language is words of affection so one way that I love to be encouraged is with a card of heartfelt words. Over the years I have saved the most encouraging cards I've received in a box I call, "My Box of Encouragement."

Pleasant words are like a honeycomb, Sweetness to the soul and health to the bones.
–Proverbs 16:24, NLT

When I have a down day, I will pull out my cards and reread them. They always recharge my spirit and fuel me with passion.

To be an encourager you'll have to be on the lookout for what people do right rather than what they do wrong. When you spot someone doing something good, tell them. Call out the good. Encourage them with it. Tell them:

*"You're amazing—more amazing than you realize."*
*"You are so talented. You have a gift this world needs."*

*"You're appreciated. We couldn't do this without you."*

Encouragement goes so much further than criticism. Too many times in the name of teaching or coaching someone, we lead with criticism and instruction rather than encouragement. But as the saying goes, "People don't care how much you know until they know how much you care."

We can improve our relationship with others by leaps and bounds if we become encouragers instead of critics.

– Joyce Meyer

When mentoring or advising others, practice giving two words of encouragement for every word of instruction or correction. There's something about encouragement that opens the heart and the spirit. Encouragement lays the foundation for building trust and rapport. If you lead in any capacity, seek to encourage those you lead, and you will be astounded by the results.

## Sweet Life Secrets

- Encourage whoever, however, and whenever and you will reap what you sow.

- When someone writes you words of encouragement, keep them! Put them in a box and pull them out whenever you're down.

- Think of someone who needs encouragement. Write down their name and one thing you can do or say to encourage them. Then go do it!

# Find Your Colony

*Surround yourself with the dreamers and the doers,
the believers and thinkers, but most of all,
surround yourself with those who see the greatness
within you, even when you don't see it yourself.*
*–Edmund Lee*

**BEE FACT**

Honeybee colonies consist of a single queen, hundreds of male drones, and 20,000 - 80,000 female worker bees.

y husband and I couldn't be on more opposite ends of the spectrum when it comes to how much time we spend socializing. I'm the outgoing extrovert who would love nothing more than to fill my days with girlfriend brunches and family gatherings. I can find just about any good reason to celebrate. Cinco de Mayo? St. Patty's Day? Taco Tuesday? Don't tempt me with a good time! You name it; if it's a day that ends in "Y", it sounds like a party to me.

Lou, on the other hand, is a homebody and enjoys simply hanging out with Aiden and I, which I love 99.9% of the time. But every now and again, I have to push him to hang out with his friends at their favorite spot—the shooting range—or take a mentor to lunch. It's not that I want the house just to myself for a time (although we mammas do like a bit of solitude every now and again!), but I know how important relationships are. Regardless of how introverted or extroverted you are, it's worth it to invest in the right relationships. Who you surround yourself with is key to your success or failure in life.

Find your colony. These are your people. Whether you refer to them as your tribe, community, or influencers—they get you! They think like you and go after dreams like you. They share your passions. Like you, they are inspired and pursuing something greater than themselves. These are your Sweet Life peeps! Surround yourself with them.

> Find a group of people who challenge and inspire you, spend a lot of time with them, and it will change your life.
> –Amy Poehler

## Building Your Colony

My husband and I have several layers to our colony. Each of these people play a pivotal part in helping us create community and fulfill our God-given calling.

**Loving Family.** We are blessed with an incredible family on both sides. My mom- and father-in-love are some of the kindest, most genuine and generous people I know. I credit my own family with much of who I am today. My parents poured so much into me growing up and continue to be some of my biggest encouragers. And my siblings....well, let's just say they constantly add the fun factor in my world. We yearly (and sometimes a couple times a year) get together in one city or another to enjoy an epic weekend of fun activities and games, delicious food, and time together. Oh....and did I mention that we even wear specially designed "Sibling Weekend" t-shirts for our outings? Yes, the Reed family love runs deep!

Not everyone shares close family ties, and if that's you, then I encourage you to find a spiritual community you can be a part of at a good church. Lou and I attend a life-giving church filled with authentic, welcoming people and wise, caring pastors. Our church family is like a second family to us, surrounding us with love, community, and support.

**Authentic Friendships.** These are the people we get to "do life with." They walk alongside us on the journey and share in our most intimate joys and sorrows. Lou and I are blessed with an amazing circle of friends.

**Inspiring Masterminds.** A mastermind is a circle of people who gather for mutual collaboration, synergy, and accountability. Being a part of a mastermind group helps my husband and I achieve greater success. The mastermind members push us to set challenging goals, and more importantly, to accomplish them. One of my favorite parts of the mastermind is when we put one of the group members in the "Hot Seat." As a group, we brainstorm one of their business goals to come up with new strategies for success. We are mutually committed to each other's success and freely share knowledge, insights, and best practices. Mastermind groups are intentionally small and usually kept to just a handful of people so that all the group members get personal attention, brainstorming, and true group accountability.

**Accountability Partners.** We have three couples we invite into the behind-the-scenes portion of our lives and make ourselves accountable to. This is where we share transparency, mutual encouragement, and friendship. They have the heart and wisdom of God and the ability to ask the tough questions. They speak into our lives for direction, correction, and protection. You can't have authentic community until you truly make yourself accountable to others.

**Wise Mentors.** These are people we study and pursue relationships with because we know they walk in wisdom and have valuable lessons to teach us. They've been where we haven't. We have business mentors, marriage mentors, and spiritual mentors. Everything changes when you tap into the power of mentorship. Through the years, they have opened doors for us, shown us shortcuts to success, and shared valuable insights about what success takes behind the scenes. We only gained this wisdom by having receptive hearts and becoming students.

> Show me a successful individual and I'll show you someone who had real positive influences in his or her life. I don't care what you do for a living—if you do it well I'm sure there was someone cheering you on or showing the way. A mentor.
> –Denzel Washington

When looking for mentors, find someone who has the heart of a teacher—someone who will challenge you, develop you, and build a sense of accomplishment in you. Avoid toxic mentors who manipulate you and pull you close merely for selfish gain.

Some of our mentors are aspirational mentors. We don't necessarily have physical access to them or know them personally, but they are influencers in the space we are passionate about. They mentor us from a distance through their books, talks, social media channels, and events. One of my aspirational mentors is Oprah. I'm inspired by the impact she has had on the world. From philanthropist to media mogul to inspired author, she's trailblazed for decades, impacting people across the globe. Although I've never met her, I glean wisdom from reading her books, following her social media, and observing closely how she creatively pioneers new ventures.

**Challenging coaches and advisors.** A coach or an advisor is very similar to a mentor but oftentimes is someone you have hired to help you achieve a higher degree of success. You can get a coach in almost any area in which you desire to achieve—life coach, writing coach, business coach, financial coach, weight-loss coach—and more. Working with someone who understands your goals as well as your blockers and frustrations, and who can coach you to overcome the challenges along the way, will keep you on track and even accelerate the pace at which you achieve your desired results.

Coaches are an investment, but the results are priceless. Never be too cheap to invest in yourself. Don't let a poverty or scarcity mentality hold you back from investing in a coach. They can be the key to unlocking the life you desire and deserve. I would never have achieved what I have without a coach, and I continue to use one to propel me forward.

To build your colony, look for people who challenge you to grow, value authenticity, and model love for God and others. And when you find them, gather them close, glean from them, and give to them. Together, you'll experience the Sweet Life with your sweet peeps. Oh...and if you decide to throw a party—call me!

# Sweet Life Secrets

- Who you surround yourself with is key to your success or failure.

- Find your colony. These are your people. Whether you refer to them as your tribe, community, or influencers—they get you!

- You can't have authentic community until you can truly make yourself accountable to others.

- When looking for a mentor, find someone who has the heart of a teacher—someone who will challenge you, develop you, and build a sense of accomplishment in you.

- Coaches are an investment, but the results are priceless. Never be too cheap to invest in yourself.

- To build your colony, look for people who value authentic community, cherish life and people, and wrap it all in love.

# Downshift Once in Awhile

*Once she stopped rushing through life,*
*she was amazed how much more life*
*she had time for.*
*–Unknown*

> **BEE FACT**
>
> The bumblebee queen hibernates during winter—neither eating nor working. Her slower rate of metabolism allows her to live for long periods of time while burning very little fuel.

For our first wedding anniversary, my husband and I took a relaxing vacation to a tropical beach destination. It was paradise! Although the all-inclusive resort had every kind of watersport you could imagine—from jet skiing to windsurfing to paddle boarding—my husband and I spent most of our days dawdling by the pool, taking long naps, reading books, writing in our journals, and resting.

Prior to this trip, my idea of a vacation was seeing every possible sight, jam packing the schedule with fun excursions, and sucking every last drop of adventure that could be had out of each day. But on this trip, for the first time in my vacation life, I craved downtime—time to do nothing, time to ponder, and to pause.

As Lou and I lay by the pool, I turned to him and said, "You know I just had an epiphany. It's okay to downshift once in a while."

For the first time, I realized not only did I enjoy a slower-paced vacation, but something within me had changed—a change that I wanted to take back with me to my everyday life. I had finally given myself permission to slow down. It was finally okay—okay to rest, okay to throttle back, okay not to juggle 50 things at once—even if that was the very thing I had prided myself on in the past. It was okay to *do* less...but that didn't mean I had to *be* less.

Can you relate? Are you that woman with an "S" emblazoned on your chest, doing it all with no time to pause? I'm here to tell you that it is okay to downshift once in awhile. It's okay to rest without feeling guilty. It's okay to give yourself permission to play. Life doesn't have to be lived at a dizzying, breakneck pace in order to achieve your goals and be successful.

Here's a parable to remember when you push yourself at a punishing pace and feel guilty about taking time off to rest. The story goes something like this...

*Two woodchoppers went into the wood to chop down trees. One woodchopper was named Tom and the other John. They were often bragging about who chopped more wood. So one day, they decided to hold a competition to determine the winner. The rules were simple—whoever chopped the most trees in a day would win.*

*So the next morning, both of them took up their positions in the forest and started chopping away at their fastest speed possible. This lasted for an hour before Tom suddenly stopped. When John realized that there was no chopping sound from his opponent's side, he thought:*

*"Ah Ha! He must be tired already!" And he continued to cut down his trees doubling his pace. Fifteen minutes passed, and John heard his opponent chopping again. So both of them carried on in this manner. John was starting to feel weary when the chopping from Tom stopped once again. Feeling motivated and sensing a victory ahead, John continued on, with a smile on his face.*

*This went on the whole day. Every hour, Tom would stop chopping for fifteen minutes while John kept going relentlessly. So when the competition ended, John was absolutely confident that he would be crowned the victor.*

*But to John's astonishment, Tom had actually cut down a great deal more wood. "How did you beat me? How could you have chopped down more trees than me? I heard you stop working for fifteen minutes every hour!" exclaimed John.*

*Tom replied, "Well, it's really simple. Every time I stopped work, while you were still chopping down trees, I was sharpening my axe."*

The same goes for you sweet friend! Know when it's time to downshift and sharpen your saw. You can hustle less and still achieve more by being intentional about when you work hard and when you rest and renew yourself.

## Give Yourself Permission to Pause

Why do we need permission to pause? Shouldn't relaxing come innately to us? It doesn't. Without question, downshifting is one of the hardest things for most women to do. Sometimes it's much more satisfying to go hard and finish a project of high intensity, crush a grueling fitness workout, or fill up our social calendars than it is to rest. We live in an age of acceleration and the world's mindset is that pushing ourselves harder and doing more will make us happier, wealthier, and wiser. Hard work is commendable and will lead to greater success, but only if there is sufficient time to rest, reflect, and refuel.

The value of sleep and rest is—at best—often forgotten, and—at worst—despised. The real truth is that a life of imbalance leads to fatigue, illness, and a lack of meaning. I learned this lesson the hard way. While working in full time ministry in my young twenties, I used to believe the lie that "sleep is for suckers" and you can hustle your way to happiness.

You've probably heard people say, "I have to stay on my grind," "Hustle hard," "sleep is for suckers," or "Sleep when you're dead." Those phrases sound catchy, but are very costly in reality. If you're not careful, the hustle mindset can rob you of your health, happiness and relationships. Take the quiz on the next page and see if you are in fact hustling too hard.

Internalize these words from Matthew 11:28-30:

*"Are you tired? Worn out? Burned out on religion? Come to me. Get away with me and you'll recover your life. I'll show you how to take a real rest. Walk with me and work with me—watch how I do it. Learn the unforced rhythms of grace. I won't lay anything heavy or ill-fitting on you. Keep company with me and you'll learn to live freely and lightly" (MSG).*

Today's culture glorifies the grind, but we are called to glorify God. He designed us to need both work and rest. In fact, He modeled this way of living for us by creating the world in six days and taking one day to rest. All throughout the Bible you can see times when Jesus took time away from the crowds to rest and to spend time with His Father. While there was always more ministry to do, more diseases to heal and more people to teach, that didn't pressure Jesus out of taking time away for solitude and prayer. God has called you to a life of grace not grind.

Don't treat life as a soul crushing treadmill. Make time for prayer, worship, stillness, and Sabbath. Make time for YOU!

## Rest for the Weary

Take note of your life. When is it too stressed? Too busy? Too fragmented? If you're wrestling with exhaustion and burnout, frustrated and fried and desperate for a break, this is for you: You're facing a critical moment; it's time to take a strategic pause.

Perhaps you're leading a major ministry or business, raising a family by yourself, or caring for a sick loved one. Taking a break seems like the last and most selfish thing you could do. I've been there myself and felt the tension. But let me assure you: resting is the best and most caring thing you can do for others. You cannot pour out of an empty cup.

Dare to slow down and use the time to reimagine new possibilities. Remember you're not pausing to quit; you're pausing to regroup, recharge, refocus, and redirect.

Take a timeout. It may be as simple as taking the day off, leaving work on time, taking a sabbatical from serving in ministry, or scheduling a real vacation. Cut back on trivial distractions—material and non-material—and instead focus on things that boost your unique sense of well-being. It starts with giving yourself permission to pause. Your family, calling, and world need you to be a whole, rejuvenated, thriving person. Remember this Sweet Life truth: Sometimes you need to downshift in life so you can upshift in your happiness and enjoyment of it.

# You May be Hustling Yourself Out of Happiness If...

**Place a check mark next to each statement that describes you.**

☐ You feel guilty for taking a break.

☐ You simply don't know how to sit still and relax—ever.

☐ You worry that someone somewhere will get ahead of you while you rest.

☐ You ignore your physical, mental, spiritual and relational needs to get more done.

☐ You ignore friends or family that are telling you that you're pushing yourself too hard and label them a hater.

☐ Your only goals are career, work, or financial goals.

☐ You ignore relationships or don't have any because you never make time for them.

☐ You keep telling yourself that your stress, anxiety and depression will go away once you reach your goal.

☐ You berate yourself for not accomplishing everything on your gigantic to-do list.

☐ You have no boundaries and work bleeds into every hour of your life.

☐ You're neglecting your hobbies and you've forgotten what fun feels like.

☐ You never feel happy about where you are.

☐ Sleep, exercise, and self-care come last on your to-do list.

☐ You can't remember when you last took a day off or took a work-free vacation.

☐ You're always frazzled and late because of your exhausting schedule.

☐ You only measure success in terms of achievements and wealth.

☐ You hate your life now but keep telling yourself it will be worth it once you achieve your goal or make your fortune.

☐ You push yourself at a punishing pace driving everyone who loves you away—including your spouse and children.

☐ God is nudging you in your spirit to slow down but you keep overriding Him.

☐ You've lost focus, lost passion, and feel burnt out but you keep telling yourself to suck it up and push through it.

☐ You're always in work mode and even if you're not, you're obsessing about how you should be.

☐ You never stop to celebrate a goal achieved and instead immediately replace it with the next milestone.

☐ Your relentless pace is causing you to be rude, angry, and lash out at other people.

*If you've checked three or more boxes, then it's time to recalibrate your perspective. I'm not bashing extra effort and hard work to meet a goal, but this should be a season not a lifestyle of burnout. Learn to rest in God and His timing and grace, rather than hustle your way to exhaustion through unbalanced and unsustainable self-effort.*

## Make Room for Margin

Life is not what happens to you in the fray of the day; life is what you choose to create through intentional downtime and purposeful pursuits. Notice I said intentional downtime. Margin in your life won't happen by chance. You must choose to pause and make downtime a priority.

Margin is what I define as the intentional space you create between your daily commitments and your daily capacity. Between your limits and your load, you must leave room for God's direction. While it may seem scary, lazy, or counterintuitive at first to create a gap in your schedule and not fill it with anything, try it. In your gap is room for yourself—room to breath and room for God to surprise you, delight you, and direct you. If you're always in the hustle and bustle, you'll miss what life is really all about. God's grace and goodness will always be revealed in the gap!

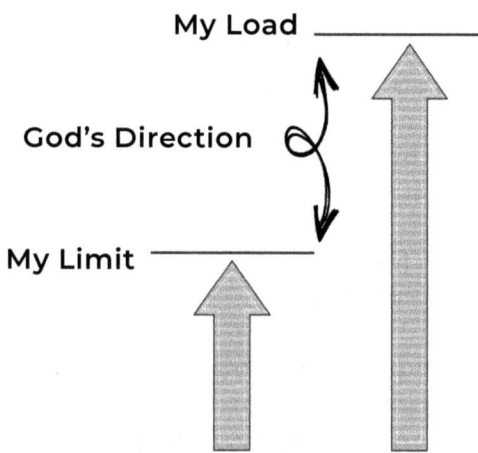

If there is one thing I've learned about myself, it's that I'm an "overscheduler." I underestimate how long things take and I overestimate what I can get done in a day or even a week. As a result I end up overextended and burning the candle on both ends. While I feel accomplished for a time, eventually I run out of steam and joy. This not only takes a toll on me, but my family as well. I've since learned that my sweet spot lies in honoring my limitations and resting in God's grace to complete the full load in His perfect timing and not my own. After all, we are created to be human beings not human doings.

Part of creating margin for yourself is to get the important things done while still prioritizing joy. You can enjoy life. Hold on; let me put that in all caps and encourage you to really internalize this: YOU CAN ENJOY LIFE! But it's a choice you must intentionally choose. Make time to go slow. Look. Laugh. Experience. Enjoy.

> Between your limits and your load, you must leave room for God's direction.

## A Cause for Pause

If you have been waiting for permission to pause, sweet friend, here is your permission slip.

You are hereby and forever more granted...

**1. Permission to Have Fun.** You have a right to carefree, happy moments, and if you haven't seen too many of them, then you're overdue for some fun. But don't wait for someone else to plan a party for you or serve up fun on a platter. Schedule fun for yourself. Right now, schedule three fun things for yourself this week.

**2. Permission to Reflect.** Pause to appreciate what you've come through and to contemplate where you're going. Schedule time in your weekly schedule to read, reflect, pray, and ponder. Capture your reflections on paper and meditate on them for new direction.

**3. Permission to be Present and Tuned in.** Be aware of what your body needs right now. Be aware of what your family needs right now. And be aware of what you need right now. Pause for a moment and simply be present. Tune into what is vital and important, not just what is urgent, excessive, or demanding. Filter out what others say is important for you and instead focus on what rings true for yourself.

**4. Permission to Rest.** There are two kinds of rest, and we need both.

Active rest is the rest that stimulates you, refreshes you, and nurtures your soul. This could include learning a new hobby, playing a sport, reading a stimulating book, taking a hike through nature, spending time in the garden, having a stimulating conversation with a friend, going somewhere new, seeking out information on your passions, or visiting a bookstore. Find something that suits you and that you enjoy. Passive rest is the second type of rest. These are the times when we need to shut our brain off and get a little escape. Passive rest could include sleeping, watching TV, reading a good novel, or doing something mindless. Be sure to have a balance of both types. Sometimes we engage in too much passive rest and not enough of the active rest that rejuvenates us.

**5. Permission to Laugh.** Downshift in your attitude and approach to life and learn to laugh. Everything doesn't have to be serious all the time. Find friends and experiences that add laughter to your life. Approach each day with a sense of humor.

**6. Permission to be Good to Yourself.** Be good to yourself at regular intervals. Schedule a massage. Get your nails done. Buy yourself something new. Splurge on something that makes you feel special. You're worth it. In the words of Tom and Donna on Parks and Rec, "Treat Yo Self!"

**7. Permission to Under-schedule.** Learn to say no to

things that overcrowd your schedule and create stress for you or your family. Leave at least one night in the week for everyone in your family to have intentional downtime. Leave at least one weekend a month pared down to the essentials and allow yourself to catch up on rest.

## Sweet Life Secrets

- Take a strategic pause to regroup, recharge, and refocus—whether it be for an hour, a day or a whole season.

- Remember, margin is the space you create between your daily commitments and your capacity. Intentionally choose to leave a gap in your schedule and day.

- Schedule a fun activity for yourself every week.

- Schedule time in your weekly schedule to read, reflect, pray, and ponder.

- Be good to yourself at regular intervals and treat yourself to something that makes you feel special.

# Keep Your Brood Happy & Healthy

*There is no doubt that it is around the family
and the home that all the greatest virtues, the
most dominating virtues of human, are created,
strengthened and maintained.
–Winston Churchill*

I'm lucky in that I married my college hero. My husband married his college crush…only in college we didn't know we would marry one another, nor were we ever girlfriend and boyfriend.

I met Lou in my sophomore year of college. The jury is still out about whether we met on campus or at church. He remembers me from church, and I remember him from the dorm. All we know for sure is that we met and became friends. I had a boyfriend at the time, but Lou was a cool guy I knew and respected highly. I admired everything about him. He was nice, outgoing, and easy to talk to. But what I liked best was that he was on fire for God and lived with integrity. While others, including myself, spent their college years partying and hooking up, Lou was passionate about knowing God and helping introduce others to Him. By the time my path crossed with Lou's, God had gotten ahold of my heart, and I was just beginning to understand what it meant to live life different than the world. And that's what struck me about Lou—it was so refreshing to see a guy who was more focused on Him than he was on me.

We both began serving in our church, which was filled with other Jesus-loving, passionate college students. Little did I know that Lou had a huge crush on me at that time, but he never breathed a word of it. Although we hung out in similar circles, the timing was never right. I had a boyfriend who I was smitten with. Lou was focused on his passion to one day go into full-time ministry and wasn't looking to be "distracted" by a serious relationship. A year later Lou left college to attend a two-year Bible school, and a few months later, I broke up with my boyfriend and the compromising relationship we had, so that I could get serious about my walk with God.

It wasn't until 18 years later when Lou and I reconnected through Facebook that I found out I had been his college crush. A random DM turned into phone conversations. Phone conversations turned into video chats (Lou lived in Phoenix and I in Dallas). Eventually though, the first date happened and, as they say, the rest is history. Two and half years and thousands of frequent flier miles later, we were happily married.

Marriage has made our Sweet Life even sweeter. When our son Aiden was born three years later, our Sweet Life soared to even greater heights. As two became three, life shape-shifted in new and interesting ways. Like a tilt-a-whirl ride at an amusement park, the highs have become higher, and the ride has been exhilarating—but at times, the unexpected twists and turns of juggling marriage, ministry, parenthood, and life circumstances can be disorienting.

Amidst the ups and downs, I've come to realize that keeping our Sweet Life from running off the rails has a lot to do with how I embrace my role within our home and family. As women, as wives, as mothers, and as grandmothers, God has given us wisdom, grace, and influence to care for our brood's health and happiness.

Your brood may or may not include a spouse, children, aging parents, roommates, relatives, or even a Goldendoodle or feisty feline. Regardless of the unique blend that makes up your household, you are the navigator of your own health and happiness and that of your family. Your family is headed somewhere, but if you are not intentionally steering it with the wisdom and grace God has given you, then you are leaving your family's outcome open to circumstance.

## Home Sweet Home

The Sweet Life begins at home, so pay attention to the home front. As a woman, God has given you an innate ability to read and regulate the temperature of your home. Like a thermostat, your attitude and outlook create the conditions that determine how cozy your home will be.

How's your home running? Is it hot and toasty from critical comments, quick-tempered reactions, and arguments that boil over? Is it cold with frosty receptions, lukewarm efforts, and lackluster family encounters? Or is it warm and cozy because you have intentionally created an atmosphere filled with loving attitudes, a spirit of servanthood, and hospitality mixed with a comforting attention and intention to cheerfully meet the needs of those in your home? God has given you the power to set the temperature in your home each day. He has provided His limitless grace for you to make the needed adjustments when you see it getting off track.

Some people are worth melting for.
–Olaf, *Frozen*

Along with your home, it's important to periodically take the temperature in your marriage. Is your love red-hot smoking or badly in need of extra sizzle? Check in with your spouse regularly. Tonight, my hubby and I went out for date night at a casual Cajun restaurant. With a live band playing behind us and bowls of gumbo before us, I casually asked him "So what do you love most about our marriage, and what is most in need of improvement?" This kicked off a great discussion in which we were able to express appreciation for one another and our life together, share insights surrounding our season as new parents, and air out areas in our communication that needed a little bolstering. We left the restaurant hand in hand and more importantly...heart in heart.

Checking in with my husband is essential to us having a happy home. We often take the temperature of our marriage and evaluate how we're doing so we can make course corrections along the way. Keeping a regular date night is a secret to our marriage sauce. As busy as life and parenting is, we need biweekly time to take a step back and invest in one another.

It's important to check in with your kids too. Take time to find out how they are doing in school, who their friends are, how their day went, and how they are feeling about things. You as a parent are their safe place, so make yourself available to be a listening ear, a reassuring voice of wisdom, and a loving bedrock for their self-worth and confidence.

One of my favorite things to do when our son was just a few months old was to see him imitate our facial expressions. This simple activity would keep my husband and I laughing as we proceeded

What can you do to promote world peace? Go home and love your family.
–Mother Teresa

to do flutter-boats with our lips, stick out our tongue, or play peekaboo. What it taught us is that kids do as they see starting at a very young age, so it's important that we are leaving our families with a positive example for them to imitate. You were given a precious gift bred into your children from day one, and that is the gift of influence. Your kids will learn from you and look up to you. So be intentional within your home and family relationships. Teach them to love God and to love others by the way you love God and love others. And teach them that they are unconditionally loved.

## How to Make Your Hive Thrive

When it comes to having a rich and satisfying home and family life, here are five key principles that we live by that have helped our hive thrive.

**1. We communicate with respect and encouragement.**

We apologize quickly and try to speak words of life and encouragement. We set a positive tone in our home with words of praise, affirmation, and celebration. Sure, we have our times of "intense fellowship"—my husband's code word for an argument—but we never lose sight of the fact that we're on the same team and our goal is to win as a family, not as individuals.

**2. We intentionally fill our house with love, learning and laughter.**

We try not to overreact, or take ourselves, or the mishaps of daily life, too seriously. Instead, we look for the blessing in each moment and choose joy along the journey. The day-to-day concerns won't matter as much as the character and confidence we instill in our children. When the little things happen, we try to step back and take a long-range view, asking ourselves, "How can I use this as a teachable moment?" Being parents later in life has taught us to roll with the punches, laugh often, and embrace love and patience. We hug our son often and let him see Mom and Dad express affection for one another.

### 3. We keep God at the center of it all.

Unless God builds our home, we labor in vain. It's important that we make time to spend with God both individually and as a family. We have a family worship and prayer night once a week and pray with our son each night before he goes to bed. We want our son to see us spending time with God and help him cultivate his own relationship with God. We train our son in the ways of God and in the love of God. We want our son to know that he is accepted, worthy, blessed, called, and unconditionally loved so he can go out in the world and share God's love with others.

### 4. We purposefully plan for work and play.

Time is precious, and with all that there is to do as a family, it doesn't happen well without a plan. While we are not overly rigid about each day, we do set a plan for the week, month, and year so that we accomplish the things that are important to us and spend quality time together strengthening our bond. Modern technology makes it easy for us to keep a digital family calendar and sync it to everyone's devices, so everyone knows what's going on. Here are a few things we schedule in.

- Weekly date nights for my hubby and me.

- Weekly family time to do something our son will enjoy.
- Time weekly to individually work on personal passion projects.
- Monthly downtime – Yes, if you want time to do nothing, you should schedule it. We fiercely protect this time. My husband especially needs periods of unscheduled time. While I love a calendar filled with activity, I respect that his tempo may not always be mine, and he needs certain days free of all plans.
- Yearly vacations – We try to take at least four vacations a year: one as a family, one as a couple, one for him and his friends, and one girlfriend or sibling trip for me.

## 5. We make good health a priority.

We strive to eat balanced meals and workout at least three times a week. We try to do active things with our kids. One of the most fun things my husband and I have done is the Spartan Race, and we look forward to the day we can compete in it with our son. While we don't buy absolutely everything organic, we strive to where we can, and we make healthy meals that are delicious. We teach our son to eat healthy snacks like fruit, nuts, and veggies. We educate ourselves about health, vitamins, and supplements, get monthly chiropractic adjustments and massages, and stay up on our physicals and other important medical exams. Health is something you either pay for preventively or in treatment, so we know it's worth it to invest in our health up front.

What will you do to make your hive thrive like never before?

## Sweet Life Secrets

- Your attitude and outlook create the conditions that determine how cozy your home will be.

- God has given you the power to set the temperature in your home each day and provided His limitless grace for you to make the needed adjustments when you see it getting off track.

- Set a positive tone in our home with words of praise, affirmation, and celebration.

- Keep God at the center of your home and family life.

- Purposefully plan for work and for play by keeping a family calendar of important goals, dates, and events.

- Make your family's health a priority with balanced meals, exercise, and healthy habits.

# Create a Hive of One's Own

*Having a home is a blessing.*
*Creating a sacred spot is happiness.*
*–Ruth Jones*

H ello, my name is Ruth, and I'm an HGTV junkie. It's true, you can think of me as obsessed with all things beautiful, organized, spacious, and inviting. I admire people who can rehab homes and repurpose junk, and there are few things I love more in this world than making a space bright, beautiful, and cozy. It makes me happy to feel "home" and to walk in a space that I have carefully curated for soul-recharging.

God created us as women to be environment shapers, nest builders, and homemakers. Not that our only place is in the home, but we possess a God-given ability to transform our environments. Sometimes amidst the flurry of making a house a home for our families, the friends we entertain, the small group we host, the homeschool we run, and the neighbors and odd assortment of people who drop by, we forget that we ourselves need room there too, both figuratively and literally.

Every woman needs a hive of her own. One of the most compelling and provoking books that I read in high school was Virginia Woolf's book, *A Room of One's Own*. In this extended essay, Woolf asserts that in order for women to write fiction, "A woman must have money and a room of her own…" Written in a time when women were fighting for personal freedom, literary equality, and access to education, I loved the concept of women needing a space of their own in order to create.

In modern times, the opportunities to create, custom, and craft our own space abound. From shared workspaces to she-sheds and from Pinterest boards to HGTV, the options and inspirations for women to have a personal space are everywhere.

> In order to be artists we need to be in our studios, in our private rooms… in our private personal space… that sacred protected space, so we can make our work. That's the only work that's worth making, right? That's the place where we can be free enough and vulnerable enough to share what we have to share.
> —Adam Leipzig

So, with all this inspiration, why do many women lack this sacred spot? The answer lies somewhere between the many hats we wear and the many needs and priorities we juggle. The reality is that it can be challenging to prioritize claiming and creating a hive of one's own.

Soapbox and microphone please…I'm here to cheer and champion every woman to intentionally carve out her own niche in the world to express her most authentic self. I'm here to remind you that whether you require a place to be crafty and clever or you're simply frazzled and need a bit of freedom, you deserve to have a place in the world that nurtures YOU! The truth is, when we create a physical space to care for ourselves, it's in that place that we become empowered and equipped with grace and strength to care for others.

I challenge you to reclaim this element of self-care in your life and dedicate a sacred spot just for you. Your hive might be an entire home, a special room, or even a craft closet. As long as it's a physical niche that you've carved out to express your truest self and passions, then it's your hive and you can claim it as your own. Remember, it's not the size nor the space that's important but the ritual of retreating to your place of grace.

It's in this place that our hearts are engaged and our purpose is cultivated. It's in this space we draw near to God and reconnect with the truest parts of ourselves, where we are refreshed, realigned, and refueled.

Say it aloud: "In my hive is where I thrive!"

Again! "In my hive is where I thrive."

## Make It Uniquely You

There are no rules or formulas to creating this space other than to remember this: your space should be a place of rest, a place of inspiration—a place where you long to be.

You might love a space that's filled with light, ample white space, and minimal design. Or you might be totally intrigued by corkboards teeming with eye-catching, awe-inspiring visuals. Your space is as unique as you are.

I love my mom's hive. It is a multi-media artist's haven. It's filled with beautiful bolts of fabric, varying in color, pattern, and texture. I love seeing all the little spools of thread in colorful arrays side-by-side, and tables strewn with paints, canvas, and watercolor brushes. Cork boards teeming with inspirational pictures and sketches adorn the walls.

My sister's hive is an art studio within her home, complete with French doors and open-faced brick walls where she can display floor-to-ceiling charcoal drawings and hang art installations. Being in her studio is like walking through a modern art museum with art in all stages of creative development.

My friend Elisa's hive is in her kitchen. She collects the latest cookware, cookbooks, and culinary ingredients to whip out five-course dinners and one-spoon wonders. Her spice treasure trove can rival that of a Middle Eastern spice market. Her kitchen is special to her because she loves cooking and uses her passion and expertise to shoot cooking podcasts, classes, and video tutorials and share them digitally around the world.

Me on the other hand…let's just say my kitchen is the furthest thing from a rejuvenating retreat. My home office is my hive. It's the place where I like to write, plan, read, and reflect. It's styled rustic industrial and features a rustic desk and sleek laptop where I work on my many passion projects. Beautiful art and photos of my family dons the walls, and I love having the curtains drawn back so light pours in.

A cozy loveseat doubles both as my prayer and Bible Study nook and one of my "sets" where I film my vlog. My prayer nook is outfitted with cozy throws, and all my Bible Study tools including several translations of the Bible, devotionals, highlighters, and beautiful journals for me to write in.

I love outfitting my space with things that trigger my desire to write. From great writing pens to bookshelves full of books on my favorite topics, to corkboards pinned with clippings related to upcoming projects, my hive is carefully curated in a way that makes me want to create. From the moment I enter the space, I am recharged, refreshed, and rejuvenated. My spirit is quieted, and God meets me there.

The right environment is a catalyst for creativity and fuels purposeful progress. Set yourself up for success. What space do you need to claim and what furniture, tools, and visuals do you need to outfit it with in order to trigger you to do what you love?

## Fashioning Your Hive

As you pursue the Sweet Life, here are some simple secrets to fashion your hive as a place you will thrive:

- **Make your environment as enjoyable and inviting as possible.** Surround yourself with the things that make you feel energized. Whether rustic chic, uber modern, or bohemian eclectic, surround yourself with an ambiance that suits you, soothes you, and stimulates you.

- **Stockpile your style.** What inspires you is unique to you—so identify what motivates and rejuvenates you and stock up. Whether you knit, journal, craft, or cook, invest in the things that bring you delight. Do you like whipping up new makeup looks and dream of being an online beauty influencer? Then, make a nook in your boudoir or bathroom to stockpile your beauty booty and shoot makeup tutorials that you can share online. Got a penchant for painting? Retrofit your garage into a studio, stock up on canvases and paints, and create a space for your inner Picasso to show up and shine.

- **Let the sun shine in.** Open the windows and let fresh air in. Sunlight is known to produce vitamin D in your body, boosting your cognitive abilities and mood and warding off depression.

- **Keep it scent-sational.** Whether you love lavender or coconut lime verbena, scent your home with fragrant candles, diffusers, or wax melts. I love all things that smell like baked goods while my husband laughingly says it only makes him hungry. He on the other hand loves all things tropical. So a piña colada candle is our happy place.

- **Choose your color palette wisely.** Colors can calm, excite, sooth, stimulate, or even stress. You don't have to take a course in color theory (although wouldn't that be fun?!), but do choose a palette that fits your vibe.

- **Keep it restful.** Remove anything from your environment that doesn't recharge you or that distracts you from the purpose of your space. Television, bills, and junk mail probably don't belong.

- **Declutter.** Clutter is the killer of comfort. Clutter invites chaos and chokes creativity. Purge your space and make sure it's clean and tidy. And for the things you choose to keep, find cute ways to store it. Invest in pretty baskets, bins, chests, or crates so you can put things away and visually declutter. Out of sight means off your mind, freeing you up to think about your creative pursuits.

Start planning your stylish hive and make it thrive today!

## Sweet Life Secrets

- You're an environment shaper. Create a hive for yourself that inspires you to the core.

- The right environment is a catalyst for creativity and fuels purposeful progress.

- Write down the kind of environment that would be uniquely you.

- Fashion your hive with things you love—including sunshine, a nice scent, the right colors and as little clutter as possible.

# Capitalize on Your Honeycomb

*The "sweet spot" is the overlap between one's greatest strength and greatest ease.*
*–Dr. Christine Carter, Ph.D.*

A honeycomb is the amazing hexagonal structure that bees build, out of wax that they produce, as a place to keep their honey.

A honeycomb is where the honey is made. You might say it's a bee's sweet spot. Well, you and I have a sweet spot too. Some people know all their lives what they want to do and what they excel at while others stumble into their sweet spot. I was more of the latter.

The only thing I've known all my life is that I wanted to succeed. It's just the way I was wired from a very young age. I remember going to a progressive school where you could work individually through the curriculum at your own speed. Each curriculum book you completed was a "pace." At the end of the school year, they held an awards ceremony where I won an award for completing the most paces in the whole school. I will never forget being called to the front of the auditorium to win a trophy that was literally bigger than me. It was so big, in fact, my Dad had to carry it. Hearing my voice called and seeing my Dad beaming as we carried out that trophy was an unforgettable moment. I knew in that moment that I wanted to feel that way all the time. If working hard led to achievement, then I wanted to work hard all my life.

My first glimpse into what my sweet spot might be happened on a random day while in high school. Les Brown was on television, delivering one of his motivational talks. As I sat glued to the television, my heart caught on fire. His talk lifted me, inspired me, and made me feel as if I could conquer the world. I remember thinking, *That is what I want to do with my life. I want to make people feel like they can conquer the world. I want to speak, and I want to inspire people.*

Although I found my calling to inspire people at a young age, my road to owning my sweet spot and walking in my calling was far from easy—and certainly not linear. Somewhere along the path to growing up, graduating, going to college, and getting a real job, I lost sight of my passion and struggled with figuring out what I was uniquely gifted to do.

In high school back in the nineties (I know, I know....I just made myself sound ancient), back in my day, there were tests to help you identify your talent. You would read hundreds of questions and bubble in a dot next to the things that sounded like what you would enjoy doing most. How much do you like organizing and sorting? Do you prefer thinking of logical, well-reasoned things? Do you like philosophical discussions about ideas? On and on it went. Your answers would then be scanned into a machine and—*poof!*—out popped a magical report that was supposed to reveal your gifts and which jobs you would be best suited for.

I was so excited to get that magical report. I was sure that it would lead me to my future success. But as I opened the pages and read down the list of suggested jobs for me, I felt like the report couldn't have been more wrong. As I read job title after job title, I thought to myself, *Did my report get switched with someone else's? This has to be a cruel joke. They think I should be a private investigator?!* Dismayed, I ditched the report, hoping I'd somehow stumble into my purpose another way.

Being achievement driven, I went to college and studied what came easiest to me—mathematics. I liked that math resulted in one right answer, and I excelled in my classes. However, I still felt unsure of where I was headed. I would pray for hours, asking God to reveal my purpose and what He created me to do. I prayed so many times through my college years that I almost felt like God was trying to keep it a secret.

I grew more and more frustrated until one day in my prayer closet, I said aloud, "Fine. If You don't want to tell me what I am supposed to do, then I'm done asking. I'm going to just do what I know to do and if You want me to be or do something else, then You'll just have to do it."

And with that, I graduated and took my first job—a customer service specialist position at a cell phone company.

There is nothing more humbling for your ego than graduating cum laude and working in a field unrelated to your degree, answering customer service calls at a cell phone company with people blowing up at you daily for their incorrect cell phone bill or their cell tower losing power—all of which you had zero control over.

I felt like a fish out of water. At my breaking point, I cried out in despair to God, and for the first time I heard clear marching orders of what I was to do next: quit my job and start volunteering full-time for my church.

*What God? How will I pay for my bills?*

Yet, I knew I had heard from God, so that Sunday, I walked up to my pastor and his wife and told them, "I am going to come by the church office on Monday morning at 8 a.m. and I would be happy to do whatever work you have for me—for FREE!" I told them I'd work so hard that they would think they couldn't live without me. How's that for 20-something confidence?! But it was God-confidence because I knew what He had instructed me to do.

On Monday, I showed up, got to work, and by the end of the day, I was offered a job. I didn't even have a title, but that job led to me editing the pastor's books. Editing led to ghostwriting their books. I became the women's ministry director and began helping plan the annual women's conference. Then I was invited to be a speaker at the conference.

Suddenly my heart was aflame again. I was doing everything I had ever wanted to do, all wrapped up in one job. I was teaching image classes, writing books, speaking at conferences, and inspiring others. Those early years of experience paved the path for what I'm doing today—walking in my true potential and abundant living and encouraging women everywhere to do the same. How I got here could only have been God, but I had found my honeycomb—my sweet spot.

## Clues to Your Calling

Finding your sweet spot doesn't have to be a winding journey if you know what to look for. Here's some clues to your calling that will lead you down the path of purpose:

Your sweet spot will:

- **Be your place of brilliance.** Everyone has one! Dan Miller, author of *48 Days to the Work You Love*, calls it a "Zone of Genius." It's your place of genius. It's unique to you—your personality and your gifts and talents all mixed with your own original approach. While others may share a similar gift, what you have to give to this world is special, and no one else can do it quite the way you would do it. It's your unique blend of awesome sauce.

- **Generate room for great joy.** You'll know when you've stepped into your purpose when you're operating from a place of joy and fulfillment despite the hardships and hard work. If you've never watched *Chariots of Fire*, I highly recommend it. It's an older flick, but it tells the story of Eric Liddell, a Scottish Olympic athlete and Christian missionary. He refused to compromise his faith and run in the pre-heats for the 100-meter because they were held on the Sabbath and instead ran the 400-meter winning an Olympic gold medal. What I love about this story is not only his deep faith and unwillingness to compromise, but also his deep passion and love for running. My favorite line from the movie is when Eric Liddell says, *"I believe God made me for a purpose, but he also made me fast. And when I run, I feel His pleasure."* When you are in your sweet spot, not only will it bring you pleasure, it will bring God pleasure.

The sweet spot is where duty and delight converge.
–Thomas Mann

After all, He created you and is the One who gave you your unique gifts and talents. He wants you to feel alive, energized, and full of passion and joy as you use them.

- **Lengthen time.** You will enter a zone where it feels like time stands still and you can do that activity for hours. When athletes enter the "zone" they talk about experiencing a place of extreme focus in the moment—a place where all worries, negative thoughts, doubt, or fear about results fade away. What do you enjoy doing that causes you to lose track of time, cares, and concerns?

- **Magnify your gifts.** What you do well comes easily to you and causes you to shine. Take a minute and assess: What do you get compliments on? What feels effortless to you that others are frequently amazed by? What do you love doing so much that you would do it for free?

- **Empower you to have massive impact.** When you begin doing what you love, it will attract people and opportunities to you. Others will begin to see that your gift is special, and it will open doors of opportunity for you.

We are given our dreams and desires for a reason. They are our portals to the Sweet Life. You will discover who you really *are* by following what you really *want*. Don't ignore the promptings, nudges and dreams tugging at your heartstrings even if it's leading you in new and unexpected directions. These are clues and cues God is sending you to lead you to a life you will love. Why settle for humdrum existence when God designed you for get-up-and-go passionate living in your sweet spot?

> Your work is going to fill a large part of your life, and the only way to be truly satisfied is to do what you believe is great work. And the only way to do great work is to love what you do. If you haven't found it yet, keep looking. Don't settle. As with all matters of the heart, you'll know when you find it.
> —Steve Jobs

## Profit From Your Passion

It's not enough to know your gifts—you must own them! It's time to harvest that honey, sweet friend! Whether you're rockin' just one talent or many, you need to own that space and cash in on your craft. Become so good at it that people seek you out for your talent and want to pay you for it.

Here's hard-earned wisdom that will help you profit from your passions:

**1. Own your vision, value, and goals.** Identify and establish for yourself what the vision for your life is and what you value. If work-life balance is important, then don't compromise just for a big title and a high-paying salary. If flexibility, creativity, and unlimited income potential are things you value, then seek out opportunities that align with those values. Don't compromise or apologize to anyone for the values you cherish. Set a goal to do what you dream of doing and then get after it, believing that God will crown your efforts with success!

**2. Play to your strengths.** What comes easy to you? What are you naturally gifted at? Where do you shine? Regardless of the position you are in, you can make it more of a dream role by seeking out projects and assignments that cater to your unique gifts and talents. Do you want to one day lead a Fortune 500 company? Then start seeking out leadership opportunities in your current role. Have a flair for interior design? Ask a few friends if they would like help refreshing a room. Build up your portfolio and skillset by hustling right where you are. It will always lead you to the next thing, which will lead you to the next thing. And let me drop this nugget in for those of you who feel stuck in life: Don't stay stuck in a position where there is no room for growth or where you're not playing to your strengths. I have been there several times in my life, and instead of feeling talented, I felt trapped. Girl, get out and move on to something else. If they can't see your shine, it's time to go where you can glow.

**3. Just say yes!** God will lead you into your sweet spot through a series of opportunities that you will need to say yes to. Most of the time they will feel inconvenient and you may at times feel scared and unqualified, but just say yes! Throughout my life, I've been asked many times to take on a role that I had no idea how to do, but I just said yes. God graced me with the wisdom to figure it out along the way, and one door always led to another. You never know which "Yes" opportunity will land you in the life you've only imagined.

**4. Be willing to work and study hard.** Once you discover your gifts, you must cultivate them. Study your craft and invest in education, books, conferences, and coaching in the area you want to excel. Read widely and research thoroughly to learn everything you can about your area of passion. Find someone who is doing what you want to do and connect with them. Work hard and practice to get better. Don't expect success to happen overnight or without any effort on your part. As the famous Vince Lombardi saying goes, "The only place success comes before work is in the dictionary." Malcolm Gladwell, in his book *Outliers*, says it takes 10,000 hours (or 10 years) of deliberate practice to become an expert at something. Be willing to pay the price to become an expert at your craft. Long-term commitment combined with high levels of practice leads to expertise. Don't stop at being good at something; become great. Even if the world doesn't notice what you're doing now, eventually your expertise will come with a payday.

> In order to do what you want to do, you've got to be around people who are doing it and in places where it's happening.
> –Ken Coleman,
> The Proximity Principle

**5. To capitalize, specialize.** Know your niche and understand your craft and your customer. Focus on the unique problem you are called to solve and your personal brand (the unique way you go about solving that problem). This is key to your increase in life. When you need to see a doctor for a specific problem, they often send you to a specialist. The specialist gets paid more than a primary care doctor because they have advanced training, degrees, and expertise in a specific area. They are clear about the value they bring and who they can help. Take what you do and specialize—turn it into a premium product or concierge service that is tailored to the people you want to work with. Get crystal clear about your own calling, customer, and personal brand. Solve a specific problem for people, get good at it and then get extremely good about telling that story. Become the best there is and make the world listen.

**6. Monetize your message.** Raise your value and visibility as an expert by learning how to monetize your message. The world is full of people who could benefit from your professional knowledge and are willing to pay you for it. Reach a wider audience and open up new streams of income by exploring new methods. Here are just a few ways you can rock your revenue and create opportunities for commerce:

- Write a book or ebook about your passion or expertise
- Create a workshop or seminar
- Teach a course at a community college on a subject you're an expert in
- Turn your professional knowledge into a consulting company or tutoring service
- Create an app related to your area of expertise
- Offer your expertise as keynote speaker for organizations, conferences or conventions
- Earn money by offering an online class, video course, or webinar series

- Start a membership-based subscription service
- Become a coach and offer individual or group coaching sessions
- Create a product to sell, whether online or in a brick and mortar stores
- Create an event around your passion, such as a fundraising event or festival
- Turn your skill into a concierge service and offer it to interested clients
- Take your expertise virtual, like a virtual assistant or virtual bookkeeper
- Create a supporting service for things people enjoy such as a repair company, restoration service, or storage provider

You can profit from your passion and turn your existing skills into new streams of revenue or simply dial into your sweet spot for greater impact and fulfillment. Whatever your motivation, the world needs what you were created for. There's something you're called to do right now, so discover it today!

# Sweet Life Secrets

- Take time to appreciate your own awesomeness. Ask yourself these questions to identify your sweet spot:

   *In past jobs, what problems have you solved?*

   *What are your proudest achievements in life?*

   *What comes naturally to you and is so easy or fun it almost seems like it shouldn't be called work?*

   *What do co-workers or friends usually compliment you on?*

   *What nice things have managers said about you on performance reviews?*

   *What cause, activity, or mission sets your soul on fire and propels you to take action?*

- You'll know when you've found your sweet spot, because you'll be operating in a place of joy.

- God will lead you to your sweet spot through a series of opportunities that you will need to say yes to.

- The unique problem you are called to solve and your personal brand (the unique way you go about solving that problem) is key to your increase in life.

# Momentum is Magical

*When you experience positive momentum,*
*you'll never want it to stop.*
*–Dan Sullivan*

A honeybee can fly for up to six miles, and as fast
as 15 miles per hour.

**M**omentum is an interesting beast. When my husband and I were newlyweds and about to celebrate our first Christmas, I told him there was only one thing I wanted for a gift, but it was going to be a big ask. I asked him to commit to working out with me on a consistent basis. I knew that I wanted to make healthy choices for my life, but I knew I would stick with my good intentions longer if I had him to help me. Up to that point, my husband had never consistently worked out in his life. He was graced with a tall, lean physique and could eat whatever he wanted without gaining a pound. But with the aim of pleasing his new bride, he promised to give me the gift of a lifetime and workout with me.

Little did he know what he signed up for. Had he known we would join Camp Gladiator and go to one of the most intense boot camp workouts, vigorously exercising for 60 minutes starting at 4:30 a.m. in the morning, he might have rethought the whole deal. But no Christmas gift take-backs!

I can still remember our first bleary-eyed morning trying to convince ourselves to roll out of bed and get dressed for bootcamp. Both of us were wondering what in the world we were doing and why had we picked such a crazy time. Lou not only didn't workout, but he was also a notorious night owl, often going to sleep at 1 or 2 a.m. Needless to say, that's not much rest when you have to roll out of bed at 4 a.m! As we suited up and scooted out to meet up with a group of 15 others, our only goal was: *Do not die.* Fifteen minutes into the warmup, we realized we may not achieve our goal. However, dripping with sweat and with Gumby legs of Jell-O, we lived through our first workout. Not only did we make it through one workout, but as of this writing, we've surpassed more than 300 workouts!

Commitment is the ignitor of momentum.
–Peg Wood

What made us stick? The magic of momentum! The more we worked out, the more we wanted to work out. It became easier every time we went. Now we wake up with relative ease at 4 a.m. and *look forward* to our early morning routine. When we don't workout, we miss it. What was once a struggle is now a system. What was once a hope has become a habit.

Momentum is like that. Like walking up a hill, it starts out hard and difficult. It takes all your willpower, intention, and effort to accomplish the smallest of results. Whether you are working on finishing a degree, trying to lose weight, building a business, or launching a dream, it feels slow. The effort is painstaking. Everything in you wants to quit, and you might feel as if you're never going to make it.

But the key to momentum is to tough it out long enough for it to kick in and take effect. Because like going up a hill, at some point in your pushing, striving, climbing, and pursuing, you are going to reach the top, and then it's all downhill from there. You're going to get over the hump, and the magic of momentum will begin. Your efforts will begin to feel easier. Your motivation will come quicker and last longer. And your results will accelerate and increase exponentially. The fruits of your effort start out small and slow then come in increasingly larger, faster returns. Rather than pushing for your goal, with momentum, your dream will begin to pull you forward

## Momentum Is Yours

Here are some essential tips about keeping your passion and your pace. Here's what I know about momentum now:

- **Momentum is essential to the Sweet Life.** Being without momentum is rough. Dreams seem lofty and unattainable. Working toward them is all toil and drudgery, resulting in start-and-stop progress—if it happens at all. This is how most people live their lives. And without momentum, results are minimal, even with tremendous effort. The Sweet Life you were intended to live is one lived with passion and pace. While hard work is required, the Sweet Life gives you an inner motivation and inspiration that continually moves you forward into abundant living.

The world is wide, and I will not waste my life in friction when it could be turned into momentum
.–Frances Willard

- **God is the author and finisher of momentum.** God intended you to fulfill the dreams He's placed in your heart, and He wants you to give you a life of momentum. That's right, I said give you a life of momentum. It's not solely based on your efforts. It's God working in you. Philippians 2:13 says, "For it is God who works in you to will and to act in order to fulfill his good purpose" (NIV). God promises He will actively be at work in you, helping you to will (resolve) and act (repetition) to accomplish His will. Not only will He supply you with fresh momentum at every turn, but He will finish the work He began in you

- **Creative visualization triggers momentum.** Lou and I start every year by creating a Vision Board of what we want to accomplish for the year. We pick up a foam project board from an office supply store and get an assortment of magazines. We then schedule a Vision Board night where we go through our magazines clipping pictures and words that speak to us about our dreams. We collage them, pasting them on our board and title our creation with a bold headline across the top that speaks to our overall theme or goal for the year. We then place our completed vision board in a high traffic area

where we'll see it often. Sometimes it's in our bedroom, our office or even on the vanity in the bathroom. By looking and meditating on these images, our mind is triggered daily with inspiration and creative ideas that move us in the direction of our dreams. This creative tool helps us see our success before we achieve it and focuses us on taking the necessary corresponding action.

- **Focus intensifies momentum.** Your life will always move in the direction of your dominant focus. The more you focus on something, the faster the momentum. Often we fail to make progress because our time and attention are spread across too many ventures. Instead, gain laser-like clarity on what one thing you need to focus on in this season and put all your effort into it. Fine-tuning focus will lead to increased momentum.

- **Progress and rewards fuel momentum.** Create daily wins and reward yourself at key milestones. Set daily goals for yourself that are highly achievable and give you a "win" for the day. The more you see yourself making progress and "winning," the more motivated you will be to keep pressing to achieve your goal. Psychologists have a term for this type of momentum: goal gradient. It means that the closer you get to your goal, the harder you will work to achieve it. Marketers understand this and build it into their rewards promotions. Ever have a food punch card offering the tenth meal free? The closer you got, the more you wanted to eat there to get your free meal. Use this strategy on your goals. Create some daily wins for yourself and establish a milestone that once reached, gives you a reward. I've even gone as far as creating my own goal punch card. Each day I take a consistent action, I get a punch or a checkbox, and when I reach my reward—it's party time!

- **Consistency multiplies momentum.** I'm a math girl at heart, so here's my equation for creating momentum that has held true in my life. Small consistent actions (A) multiplied by repetition (R) over time (T) eventually compound and create massive momentum (M) in your life.

$$A \times R \times T = M$$

Action x Repetition x Time = Momentum

Consistently applied, this leads to what I call it "The Cycle of Success." Repetition—taking consistent action toward your dreams—boosts results. Getting results strengthens your resolve. Stronger resolve increases your repetition, which in turn gets you greater results. It's a cycle that gets easier and turns faster the more you do it, making momentum and dream achievement your way of life.

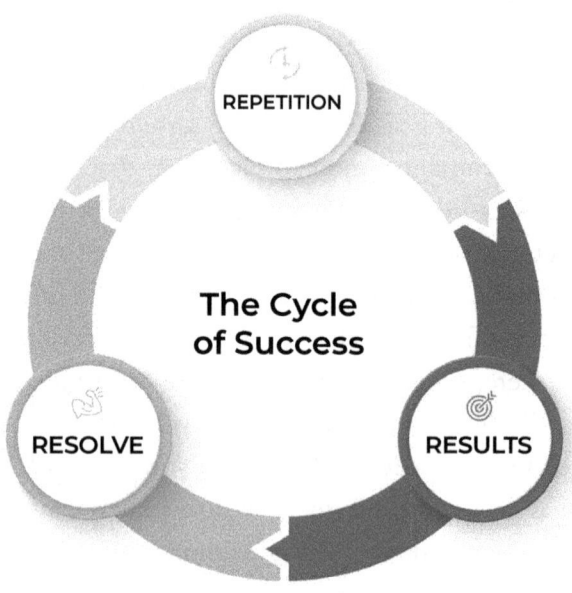

I'm not sure what your dreams are and what you might be working on (or maybe have given up on), but I want to encourage you today: As a child of God, momentum is yours. This is what I declare each morning: I wake up, look in the mirror and boldly declare, "Momentum is mine." Then I go after my goals and pursuits for the day, expecting God to help me to will and to do. When I feel my resolve and my repetition waning, I pray and ask God for His strength and say aloud, "Momentum is mine."

So whether you're launching a ministry, working on weight loss, or studying for your MCAT exams, let God work the power of momentum in you. Climb, press, pursue, and keep doing it—past your peak, past the point where you want to quit. And then lean in and let God carry you over and onward to your Sweet Life.

Keep moving ahead because action creates momentum, which in turn creates unanticipated opportunities.
–Nick Vujicic

# Sweet Life Secrets

- Momentum is essential to the Sweet Life. God intended you to fulfill the dreams He's placed in your heart, and He wants you to give you a life of momentum.

- God is the author and finisher of momentum. Not only will He supply you with fresh momentum at every turn, but He will finish the work He began in you.

- Focus intensifies momentum. Your life will always move in the direction of your dominant focus.

- Progress and reward fuel momentum. Create daily wins and reward yourself at key milestones.

# Mind Your Own Beeswax

*Sweep in front of your own door.*
*–German Proverb*

**BEE FACT**

Secreted from glands, beeswax is a waxy material produced by worker bees and used to build honeycomb. Today beeswax is commonly used in drugs, cosmetics, artists' materials, furniture polish, and candles.

If you've spent any amount of time on a playground, chances are you've heard a child pointedly tell another to, "Mind your own beeswax!" No one knows for certain where this phrase came from, but according to some popular myths, the expression might have its origins in a time when people sealed their letters with beeswax so no one could read them. Others think it derived from the colonial period when women would sit by the fireplace making wax candles together. Whatever the origin, it's clear that when uttered, someone is telling you to mind your own business and respect their privacy.

A key ingredient to living the Sweet Life is learning not to meddle in the affairs of others without invitation. I'm the first to admit, it can be tempting to get involved in something that doesn't concern you, whether out of sheer curiosity, a pinch of nosiness, or even genuine concern and compassion. However, there is a big difference between trying to help someone and being a busybody.

Proverbs 26:17 tells us, "He who passes by and meddles in a quarrel not his own Is like one who takes a dog by the ears" (NKJV). Sooner or later, you're going to get bitten. Or as I like to put it—meddle in others' beeswax and you're sure to get stung!

Ask yourself: Are you easily tempted to get involved in the affairs or dramas of others? Do you take on other people's quarrels, problems, or stress as your own? Learn to live drama-free. You will have fewer negative interactions and more positive conversations and relationships.

People shouldn't feel free to constantly air their problems and toxic thoughts in your presence. That's not being a good friend; that's being a dumping ground. You shouldn't be everyone's therapist and take on their problems unless you're licensed and getting paid for it.

When it comes to drama, one of my sister's favorite phrases is, "Not my circus, not my monkeys." When either of us get buried under a mound of problems and start to lose perspective on our own boundaries, we remind each other of this phrase—and to let the drama go. Certain things are outside of our control and truly not our problem. Give it a try.

Say it aloud now: "Not my circus, not my monkeys!"

Doesn't that feel good? After all, we all like to see a good circus, but who wants to bring the circus home and live with the monkeys? That's not the life you were called to live.

So why do we get caught up in others' circus acts? We need look no further than the big top for the answer. Ringmasters thrive for the spotlight and live to be the center of attention and action. In other words, they live for chaos and drama. But sweet friend, that's not you. Don't be trapped by meddling mindsets. Recognize them and ask God to change them in you.

## Meddling Mindsets

So why do we meddle in others' affairs? There are several reasons it's so tempting:

- We like feeling wanted and needed by others.
- We crave approval and the feeling of worthiness and acceptance from trying to rescue others.
- We like the excitement that drama and strife generate.
- We think problems give us a purpose and a reason for being.
- Drama helps distract us from our own lives and taking the necessary action to deal with our own problems.
- We think we know what is best for everyone else and must help them realize it.
- We struggle with a Messiah Complex and feel responsible for fixing everything.
- We are unwilling to trust other people and their situations to God.
- We feel we must shield people from their own mistakes, consequences, and failures.

These mindsets will not only keep you trapped in a negative, drama-filled life, but your good intentions may also eventually alienate you from others.

God has not called you to be the end-all-be-all to everyone's problems and situations. Only He can fill that place. We would do well to remember His role and our role. Our role is to intercede,

Make it your goal to live a quiet life, minding your own business and working with your hands, just as we instructed you before.
–1 Thessalonians 4:11, NLT

encourage when we can, and advise with wisdom and restraint—not to fix every problem or get involved with every distraction. His role is to be the ever-present, Helper, Mighty Deliverer, and Savior.

## Drama vs. Distraction vs. Divine Leading

When it comes to getting involved with others' affairs, there is a big difference between drama, distractions and divine leading.

- **Dramas are draining.** They cost you time, energy, and emotions. They are toxic.

- **Distractions are delaying.** They cost you time and effort better spent elsewhere and often lead to detours. They are hindering.

- **Divine leadings are fulfilling.** They may cost you in terms of time, energy, resources, or emotions, but they *always* return more than they give. They are rewarding and God orchestrated.

Minding your own beeswax doesn't mean shirking responsibility, adopting a blanket "it's not my job," or "it's not my problem" attitude. It doesn't mean becoming callously indifferent to the plight or sufferings of others. It means being Spirit-led when getting involved in others' affairs.

Learn to balance the Law of Compassion with the Law of Restraint. The Law of Compassion encourages us to care for those who are down-trodden, be compassionate, listen and extend wise counsel, and even physically and financially help as God prompts us.

Remember the story of the Good Samaritan? He took on another's problems and was praised by Jesus as an example of how to love others. However, it's wise to balance godly compassion with godly restraint. If you don't feel a wise tug on your heart to get involved, then don't. Practice restraining yourself from passing judgment, giving unsolicited advice, airing your opinions, or getting involved in more permanent ways, like lending money, if your spirit is sending up red flags. An ounce of restraint and foresight can be the best protection and heavenly hindsight.

Maybe you consider yourself a nosy Nancy, a drama magnet, or a faithless fixer. How do you turn over a new leaf? Here are some simple steps you can use to properly evaluate whether or not to get involved in someone else's affairs. Ask yourself these five questions:

1. Is this a divinely prompted opportunity or opening?
2. Do I have peace about being involved? Or is guilt, obligation, fear, worry, or a need for acceptance driving my involvement?
3. What will it cost me?
4. What are the boundaries, whether mine or someone else's, that I need to recognize and respect? Remember, everyone is entitled to their own privacy, opinions, decisions, beliefs, values, and mistakes.
5. Have I been invited to get involved or give my opinion? What is my relationship with this person?

If your involvement passes this 5-question litmus test with flying colors, then lend a hand. If not, take a pause for the cause and step back to better evaluate others' boundaries and your own.

## Benefits of Healthy Boundaries

When you learn how to mind your own beeswax— balancing compassion with restraint and establishing healthy boundaries—you will:

- Have more peace and less drama and strife
- Make progress in your own life
- Have more positive relationships and conversations
- Get involved at the right time, making an eternal impact in the lives of others
- Be counted as wise and earn others' respect and confidence

Sweet friend, don't settle for the circus when you can have the Sweet Life!

## Sweet Life Secrets

- Know when to remind yourself, "Not my circus, not my monkeys!"

- Be spirit-led when getting involved with other's affairs.

- Practice the Law of Restraint when passing judgment, giving unsolicited advice, or airing your opinions.

- Practice the Law of Compassion when prompted by God to show love to others, give wise counsel, or lend a helping hand.

- Take time to evaluate before getting involved.

# Be Ridiculous at Least Once

*When in doubt, be ridiculous.*
*–Sherwood Smith*

What do you call a bee having a bad hair day?
A frizz-bee.

L ooking back, I have to admit: It was a little ridiculous.
Lou and I were in the Bahamas celebrating our one-year
anniversary. Something that has always been on my bucket list
was to swim with the sharks in a cage. However, this boat trip
would take me far beyond that. As we bopped out to the center
of the ocean, we pulled anchor. Our boat guide dropped a
bloody bait box in the water to the ocean floor. Within minutes
over 30 Caribbean Reef sharks stormed the area, swimming
circles around the boat. Slowly our guide let a rope drop in the
water and offered the opportunity for those who wanted to,
to get in the water with a snorkel and mask and hold onto the
rope. We were told not to make any sudden movements, get sick
in the water, or swim off on our own. Swimming with a pack of
sharks—no cage, with bait and blood in the water, and trusting

that the other 10 people in the water didn't do anything stupid to risk the life of the group was…ridiculous.

From the safety of my cozy couch, I think back to how crazy of an idea it was, but it was also incredibly adventurous, exhilarating, and exciting. And not too bad of a story to tell my future grandkids either. I've got senior citizen bragging rights!

It wasn't the first time I had talked my husband into being a little ridiculous with me. While dating, I took him on a surprise skydiving trip for his birthday. And I'm sure it won't be the last either.

Merriam Webster defines ridiculous as "arousing or deserving ridicule; extremely silly or unreasonable; absurd, preposterous." The antonym or opposite of ridiculous are words like serious, sensible, reasonable. With this definition, who would want to be ridiculous?

It's human nature to want to fit in, to be taken seriously, and to be accepted. To be ridiculous would be to risk being rejected, ridiculed, or even be labeled a joke.

But…

- *What if* not being sensible led you to a new discovery or a new hobby or caused you to reach out to a new person?
- *What if* you intentionally chose to be silly instead and laughed more, not taking yourself or others so seriously?
- *What if* you remembered that to be alive meant to be full of life? What if it led you to an exciting life change or new discovery?
- *What if*, instead of working late or eating lunch at your desk, you decided to see where a trail in the woods led or *what if* you sat by a pond and lost yourself in a good book?

If all those things are possible, then being ridiculous might be just what you need to step into the Sweet Life.

## A Ridiculous Sight

One person I know who's not afraid to be a little ridiculous now and then is my mom. She certainly knows how to bring out the levity in life.

Back before 9/11, when going to the airport and standing outside the gates to wait on the passengers was possible, my mom gathered her three siblings and a spouse-in-law to pull off a birthday surprise for her sister's 60th birthday. Dressed in full costumes with big character heads, they went to the airport as Mickey Mouse, Bugs Bunny, a gorilla, a chicken, and Winnie the Pooh. They stood outside my

There's power in looking silly and not caring that you do.
–Amy Poehler

aunt's arrival gate, holding huge Happy Birthday banners and passed out slips of paper to everyone, asking the crowd to sing Happy Birthday as my aunt got off the plane.

As she walked down the sky rail bridge, she saw the most ridiculous sight. A huge crowd was singing, "Happy Birthday, Patsy," led by a chicken doing the chicken dance, a gorilla beating his chest, a laughing Bugs Bunny and Mickey and Pooh, and a chicken holding the signs. After the costumed hats came off, revealing her siblings, she doubled over from laughter with tears running down her face. Later she joked that she didn't realize they were singing to her and instead thought there was another Patsy on the plane! Yes, this story goes down in the family's Ridiculous Moments history books!

## Being Ridiculous Rocks

Here's a Sweet Life Truth: you're never too old or too young to break the social norms and live a little.

Helen Ruth Elam Van Winkle, otherwise known as "Baddie Winkle," is someone who has the courage and vivaciousness to be ridiculous. At 90 years old, she dresses in flamboyant and outlandish outfits and posts them on Instagram.

It all began with a fun photo taken by her great-granddaughter in 2014. Baddie had dressed in jean shorts and a tie-dye shirt, and her daring daughter posted it online. In just a month and thousands of shares later, she was the newest social influencer with companies calling and asking her to wear their brands.

Now Baddie's Instagram feed boasts photos of the world's coolest grandmother rocking the latest hip trends from neon technicolor trench coats to a sassy, Tweety bird swimsuit.

Today, she has almost 4 million followers on Instagram, nets $2500–$5,000 a post and is paid to endorse products and clothes. Beyond that, she has inspired the elderly to have the courage to express themselves and do the things they enjoy. It just goes to show that being ridiculous can be not only fun, but also profitable. So, embrace your quirkiness!

Mix a little foolishness with your serious plans. It is lovely to be silly at the right moment.
–Horace

Sometimes we just need to lighten up and loosen up. God created us to laugh, have fun, and be adventurous. Even God has a sense of humor—how else can you explain the silly things children do, that weird person at work or family gatherings (who will remain nameless), or all the strange, unique varieties of animals we have on earth? Ever heard of the Chinese Water Deer that have no antlers but really long fangs? It's ridiculous and looks more like a vampire than a deer. God must have been having a bit of fun creating that one.

Jesus' first miracle was one of leisure and luxury, turning water into wine at a wedding. If God's son could take time to do something out of the norm just to be a blessing, then so can you!

## Being Ridiculous Builds Resilience

The more you exercise your silly, adventurous side—embracing the unexpected in small things—the more resilient you are when big, unexpected things in life come along.

In Charles Duhigg's book, *The Power of Habit,* he tells the story of Lisa. She was a participant in a scientific research study about people who had destructive habits that they turned around in a remarkably short time. Amid facing one of life's biggest blows—her husband having an affair and leaving her—she chose to be ridiculous. She decided to trek through the desert in Egypt. At the time Lisa, a chronic smoker, was broke, struggling with obesity, and reeling from her husband's affair. That ridiculous idea turned into a goal that motivated her to quit smoking and begin running so she would have the stamina to trek through the desert. Eleven months later, she took that amazing desert trek accomplishing her goal. Three years after that, she ran a marathon, bought a house, started her master's degree, and got engaged. Her ridiculous goal reaped audacious results.

Sometimes the first step in making a lasting life change or overcoming life's worst blows means embracing your own big, bold, ridiculous idea.

Being ridiculous doesn't mean losing all sense of responsibility, wisdom, or safety. It simply means that every once in a while, you color outside the lines and investigate new possibilities. Taking a new out-the-norm action requires that you have confidence in yourself. With time you learn that if things go sideways, you're able to figure it out, adapt, and go with the flow.

Do something ridiculous and you may just see God do something miraculous.

–Jabin Chavez

People will not always "get you" when you choose to do something outside of the norm. I don't know about you, but the older I get, the less I care about who doesn't "get" me—and you shouldn't either.

Want to color your hair blue just once or cut it all off? Go for it. It's only hair. It will grow back. Want to go backpacking across Europe or skydiving on every continent? It's your world, go for it!

Be ridiculous. The memories, the laughs, and your stories of adventure will be some of the things you cherish most.

You only get this one wild and precious life to live, so make it a good one. I want some of my last words of wisdom imparted to my children's children to be: *Love God and remember to have fun.*

## Sweet Life Secrets

- Try something unexpected.

- Shake things up in your morning or evening routine. Do you always come home, eat, and watch TV to unwind? Instead, go for a walk or try playing a board game with your roommate or family.

- Take a new route to work.

- Order something totally out of your comfort zone when dining at a restaurant or pick a new cuisine you've never experienced (Ethiopian, Mediterranean, Indian, Argentinian—the possibilities are endless).

- Take an unplanned trip or go on a spontaneous date.

- Go on vacation without an itinerary. Go with the flow and explore. Like the looks of a restaurant along the way? Try it. Even if it turns out totally awful, at least you will have a great story to tell.

- Try to meet at least one new person each day.

- Update your look or rock a new style you've been too afraid to try.

- Sing at a karaoke bar, broadcast live on social media, or try stand-up comedy.

- Shop for groceries somewhere new. If you haven't shopped in a Mexican, African, or an Asian grocery store, go explore.

# 18

# Be Sweet to Yourself and Others

*Three things in human life are important.*
*The first is to be kind. The second is to be kind.*
*And the third is to be kind.*
*–Henry James*

BEE FACT

Date honey contains a higher ration of fructose to glucose than bee honey making it sweeter than bee honey.

T here are two people who most need you to show them some kindness:

1. Yourself
2. Everyone else!

The world—including yours—could use a little more kindness. Everyone has experienced one of "those days" when nothing goes right. Perhaps you dropped the ball or failed miserably at something. Maybe you had to deal with a tough client, the unexpected nail in the tire, or the baby that decided to throw up on you as you were on your way out the door. Whatever mistakes, mishaps, misfortunes, or mountains you've had to face, you deserve some kindness. You could benefit from someone offering a helping hand, a sympathetic word, or your favorite drink at Starbucks. What about an undeserved, "Don't sweat it…I still think you're awesome," or a "Don't quit, you've got this!"

It's nice when kindness comes from others, but we also need to give this gift to ourselves. Be sweet to yourself regardless of whether you've met your big goal, finished your to-do list, or ordered that tempting burger at lunch instead of a salad. Choose to love your quirky personality and laugh at your own jokes even when others don't get them. Create space for enjoying life by giving yourself the night off to read a good book rather than do laundry. I don't know about you, sweet friend, but I need this serving of sweetness every day!

> He who sows courtesy
> reaps friendship, and
> he who plants kindness
> gathers love.
> –St. Basil

Practice self-mercy. Self-mercy is when you unconditionally accept yourself and grant yourself grace with no strings attached. When you fall short of your ideals, can you make allowances for your humanity rather than hold yourself to an expectation of perfection? Self-mercy silences the inner self-critic, mounts the defense of your worth, and chooses to pick up the pom poms to cheer you on.

A little kindness and grace given to ourselves goes a long way. It teaches us to respect our own humanity, self-worth, and dignity. But what's more: our ability to show mercy to ourselves is critical to our ability to show mercy to others.

## Quick to Mercy

Wherever you are, create a forgiving environment. I once worked a job where mistakes were not tolerated. Even the smallest mishap was treated as a massive interrogation and at the end of it, someone was getting figuratively "nailed to the cross." An atmosphere like that breeds adversarial work relationships and a fear-based work environment. Needless to say, it was very stressful and no fun to work there. Make sure you are not fostering that kind of environment around yourself.

Instead, look for ways to encourage mutual success and wins for others. Seek paths of cooperation and fairness. The Bible teaches us to prefer others before ourselves. When you look for ways to do that, you will be surprised at the opportunities God opens for you.

Be quick to show others mercy and be generous in grace. Forgive quickly and don't hold grudges. Assume the best about others. Be willing to give mistakes, faux pas and careless wrongs a pass, covering over them with love and grace rather than offense, hurt or retribution. No, everyone will not deserve it, but if you are rich in mercy toward others, that mercy will come back to you, in your time of need, multiplied many times over.

One of the most difficult things to give away is kindness; it usually comes back to you.
–Anonymous

None of us are perfect and we all need a pardon from time to time. So be quick to give others a "Get Out of Jail Free" card. After all, that's what Jesus did for us. He gave us the ultimate "Get out of Jail Free" card by taking our punishment on for Himself and granting eternal forgiveness for those willing to accept it. Follow suit and be liberal in granting others mercy.

## Let It Go

Let the little things go and you will enjoy the Sweet Life more. If we harp on minor incidents, we risk coloring our relationships with the memory of the minor when we have so much greater good to offer to one another. Whatever we spotlight and focus on will grow. Let's be in the business of looking for one another's best qualities and shining moments.

Don't waste energy being upset and striving over things that can be easily overlooked. Some things are simply not worth getting bent out of shape over, and the gracious thing to do is to simply overlook it. We all experience unimportant irritations, and things others say or do can rub us the wrong way—but it's important to remember that sometimes we rub others the wrong way as well.

The Bible says we must each carry our own load of oppressive faults and bear them with patience and understanding. When you remember you are carrying your own baggage, you will be more gracious when you trip over the baggage of others.

I learned this well when I became a new parent. It's funny how having a baby can change your perspective about so many things. One of those perspective shifts was the crying baby on an airplane. Prior to having a child, I felt like I was always placed near a crying child on an airplane. It's like the cosmos was out to get me. I've had kids kick my seats relentlessly, scream at the top of their lungs for what seemed like hours, and have even had one toddler toss their daddy's coffee on my lap. More than once, I thought, "they need to get their kids under control!"

Then I had my own child. Well, whoops. What a perspective shift! Suddenly I realized so much that kids, especially babies, do is beyond their parent's control. Yes, you can teach them good manners, but at the end of the day, our little cuties need a whole lot of grace…and so do their frazzled, exhausted parents. I now extend a smile, a sympathetic word, and even a hand to a parent who needs a bit of calm in the chaos.

Remember, someone somewhere is having a worse day than

you. If you keep this in mind, it will awaken your appreciation for life and help you respond to others with more grace.

As I write this chapter, I have a coworker who recently lost her stepmother, and within a week, her father passed away. The doctor medically termed it "a broken heart." I have several friends trying to get pregnant without success, one friend who was recently downsized, and another who has been applying for countless jobs with no callbacks. You don't have to know someone's back story to be sweet, but each of these are my own personal reminder that everybody can use more kindness. You never quite know what someone might be going through.

> Be kind, for everyone you meet is fighting a hard battle.
>
> –Philo

Let's start a kindness campaign and mercy revolution. Let's go on the lookout for ways to be sweet to ourselves and others and see if we can't make this a better, sweeter world for everyone.

## Sweet Life Secrets

- Practice self-mercy every day. Unconditionally accept yourself and grant yourself grace with no strings attached.

- Look for ways to encourage mutual success and wins for others.

- Assume the best about others and be willing to give mistakes, faux pas, and careless wrongs a pass. Cover over them with love and grace rather than offense, hurt, or retribution.

- Don't waste energy being upset and striving over things that can be easily overlooked.

- Be in the business of looking for other people's best qualities and shining moments.

- Create a list of ways you can intentionally be sweet to others this week.

# 19

# Overcome the Things that Sting

*Being challenged in life is inevitable,*
*being defeated is optional.*
*–Roger Crawford*

Wasps, yellow jackets, and hornets can sting people multiple times because their stinger has no barbs on it and can be retracted. The honeybee has a barbed stinger that remains in the victim's skin with its venom sack attached.

L ife is full of things that sting.

January 1 was one of the most painful days of my life. What was supposed to be one of the most celebrated, anticipated days of the year—a day of new beginnings, a day of fresh starts and exciting possibilities—found my husband and I in the emergency room. I sat in a thin hospital gown and bled uncontrollably as we lost our first baby.

Thoughts ravaged my mind: *How can this be? How can something I had been praying for and believing for end in a miscarriage? Why would God allow this?* The pain and the sting of this loss was so acute and sharp, I was sure I'd be swallowed up by grief.

We've all felt pain. We've experienced the sharp barbs of life, whether it was the loss of a loved one, a devastating rejection, a shameful failure, a personal attack ... the list goes on. There are those hurts and hardships that are an expected part of life, and then there are those stings that we don't understand at all or see coming—the betrayal of a loved one, a senseless tragedy, or a depression from which there seems to be no end.

How do we deal with the pain? What do we do when the unexpected happens, and our world is shattered by a burden too difficult to bear? In that place, remember these three truths:

**1. Nothing is beyond God's grace to redeem, restore, or repair.**

There's no situation too difficult, too dark, too broken, too far-gone, too shameful, or too unexpected that God can't step in and redeem it. God came to heal our broken places and turn them into places of beauty. In Isaiah 61:3, God promises, "To all who mourn in Israel, he will give a crown of beauty for ashes, a joyous blessing instead of mourning, festive praise instead of despair. In their righteousness, they will be like great oaks that the LORD has planted for his own glory." God has a great exchange for you. He wants you to trade in your pain and despair for His promise of beauty, joy, and praise.

Don't allow rejection, depression, and other stings to hijack the potential of the Sweet Life story God still has for you. Things might not have started off well for you in life, or some disappointments along the way may have detoured you a bit—but it's not over. You're not finished. Please know this: it's never too late to live the Sweet Life God has prepared in advance for you to live.

**2. Whatever pain, tragedy, or brokenness you face, God never intended for you to stay stuck in it.**

We all go through painful experiences and seasons of pain, but what's worse than getting stung is getting *stuck*. Getting stung is a part of life, but getting stuck is a choice. *Refuse* to stay stuck.

Right now, you might feel that you're at your lowest point. You may feel shaky and beaten down. The wind may have been knocked out of your sails or you may even feel as if your hope is shipwrecked. Allow the presence of the Holy Spirit to come in like a breeze to comfort you and lift your spirits. Let the gentle wind of hope and the knowledge that God still has a purpose and a plan for your life buoy your faith in this moment. God has a future for you. He has an expected end that is good for you. Let hope into your heart and start dreaming again.

Life's challenges are not supposed to paralyze you. They're supposed to help you discover who you are.
–Bernice Johnson Reagen

You can start to move from where you are to where you want to be just by tapping into the grace and strength of God and taking the smallest step of faith forward. You might not feel like you have a future, but those feelings will change once you start moving. You are stronger than you think. Stand up and begin again.

Take ground. In fact, take the high ground! Climb to the heights by spending time in prayer asking God to show you His point of view. He will lift you up and set your feet on high places. When you draw close to God in the midst of your situation, God will give you a fresh, mountain-top vision for your life. As you step into the spirit, you will begin to see a bigger picture and gain a better perspective than you could get in the valley of despair.

The enemy of your soul wants you to wallow in the trenches. But sweet friend, you were called to the high ground. Look up. Step up. Climb up. You were called to reign on the mountains.

**3. What was meant for bad can be repurposed for good.**

God has the ability to turn the very things that sting, and the enemy's intent to harm and destroy you, into a Sweet Life story.

The Bible recounts a man named Joseph who experienced one tragedy after the next. He was kidnapped by his brothers and sold into slavery. After years as a loyal slave, he was falsely accused of rape and put in prison. From slave to prisoner, life was certainly moving in the wrong direction. But God still had a plan.

After interpreting a dream for the king, Joseph was freed and promoted to second in command of Egypt. When famine struck the land years later, Joseph was in a position to implement a harvesting strategy that not only saved the entire nation from starvation, but his brothers—the very ones who had betrayed him years earlier—and father as well.

Sometimes when you're in a dark place, you think you've been buried, but actually you've been planted.
–Christine Caine

Joseph had this to say in Genesis 50:20: "You intended to harm me, but God intended it all for good. He brought me to this position so I could save the lives of many people." (NLT).

What you are going through is not without purpose. You are not a failure. You are not forgotten. Your life still has meaning. You still have a purpose, and you are called and selected for an awesome finish.

God has a plan for you to use the stings that you've experienced to help encourage and bring healing to others.

Your tragedy will be used for good. There is purpose in the pain and a testimony after the test that will help set others free.

On January 1, my husband and I lost our first child. And while that broke our hearts, even as we grieved, we continued to believe God for a baby. Two months later we got pregnant again, and Aiden, our beautiful 7-pound, 10-ounce son was born in November of that same year. God birthed life amid despair and brought destiny out of difficulty. And to add joy on top of joy, God has used that experience to encourage and strengthen many others who have had miscarriages or experienced unexpected hardship.

> Sometimes good things fall apart so better things can fall together.
> –Marilyn Monroe

Starting over afresh and anew may not be easy. It may seem a little scary, but your hope can be restored. Your dreams and your life may look different than what you expected, but they are not over. Every bitter thing can be made sweet again.

As you allow God to transform your tragedy into triumph, here's a simple yet powerful action plan that will help you get started overcoming life's stings. Start with these four questions:

**1. What does an awesome future look like for you?** Name it and define it.

**2. What has been holding you back?** Fear? Bitterness? A self-perceived limitation or a lie that your dream is finished? Discredit it. Going forward, this thing no longer has the power to hold you back. You are taking your God-given power back.

**3. What new action can you take to move forward?** Pinpoint it but make the action step deliberately small. Small positive actions will move you forward faster than fantasies of gargantuan overnight change. Intentionally crawl before you walk, and you will end up sprinting in the long run. It's called the long run for a reason.

**4. Who can you be accountable to?** Share your answers to the first three questions with them and ask them to help you take your action steps and pray for you as you move forward.

Every bitter thing the enemy meant for your destruction God can repackage for your destiny. Let this truth inspire you to keep moving forward toward the Sweet Life that is *still yours*.

## Sweet Life Secrets

- There's no situation too difficult, too dark, too broken, too far-gone, too shameful, or too unexpected that God can't step in and redeem it.

- When you draw close to God in the midst of your situation, God will give you a fresh, mountain-top vision for your life.

- God has the ability to turn the very things that sting, and the enemy's intent to harm and destroy you, into a Sweet Life story.

- There is purpose in the pain and a testimony after the test that will help set others free.

# 20

# Be Brave

*She who is brave is free.*
*–Anonymous*

> **BEE FACT**
>
> The Japanese honeybee has come up with an ingenious way to kill larger insects that pose a threat to their hives, like the wasp. If an intruder is nearby, the honeybees will plot to ambush the unwanted visitor. The bees attack the predator by forming a "bee ball" around it and begin flapping their wings to create an intolerable, deadly, environment for the predator. Heat and carbon monoxide from the rapid wing-flapping suffocate and kill the intruder.

At times I've considered myself brave, and at other times, I have been the furthest thing from it. In fact, I can even recall a particular day in which I made a quite emphatic speech to my sister over the case for being less brave—the case for being average.

I was two months into pregnancy. I had started to feel the first trimester fatigue. I passionately asked my sister, "Why do I have to do something MORE? Why can't I just be pregnant and happy and enjoy this? Why can't I just be tired and sit on the couch and binge watch TV and enjoy my husband and my life? Why do I even have to aspire to write a book? Or strive for my dreams? Why can't I just enjoy being *comfortable*?"

I went on to say that my pregnancy was fatiguing me a bit. But truthfully, I *wanted* to be tired. I *wanted* an excuse to not have to reach for my dreams. The thought of having to finish my book and face the possibility that it might not be good enough was so terrifying that I wanted an excuse for never writing it and being brave.

> Don't be afraid of your fears. They're not there to scare you. They're there to let you know that something is worth it.
> –C. JoyBell C.

After listening to my passionate ranting, my sister told me a story. Just a week earlier she had been at a swim meet talking with a woman. She and this woman had often spent time at the meets but had never waded beyond small talk into deeper waters. Observing that the woman was a kind soul around 10 years her senior, a thought struck my sister about asking this woman for advice. She asked her what advice she would give her late-30, early-40-year-old self.

The woman answered, "Whatever it is you have always wanted to do, do it now." *Do it now.*

"That's why you need to write your book and be brave," my sister told me. "One day will come when you'll look back and wish you'd gone for it." I would wish I'd been brave. Of course, she was right.

Although I was about to start a new adventure and embrace motherhood for the first time in my forties, I still had deep dreams in my heart of being an author and a speaker. If I was going to go for it, I needed to start *now*. I needed to be brave. I had the wisdom of years behind me, but still the vitality of my youth. So, I must be brave.

And I was. Thankfully, with the grace of God and the grit

to preserve, that is the very reason you hold this book in your hands. It's my tangible way of reminding you too that you must be courageous enough to face your fears and brave enough to pursue your dreams. It's always worth it.

## Choosing to Be Brave

When most people think of bravery, they think of the grand gesture or a daring feat. But courage is developed in the day-to-day moments of our lives. We can train ourselves to be brave by exercising courage in the small things and accomplishing small things although we're afraid. It may mean speaking up in a meeting when you'd rather sit silent or volunteering to lead the PTA when your insides are jiggling like Jell-O, wondering if

Life shrinks or expands in proportion to one's bravery.
–Anais Nin

you have what it takes to pull off planning the spring dance. Being brave is a choice and one that must be made daily. We either retreat or advance, depending on the choice we make.

Some of the bravest people are those who succeed in the face of problems, failure, and losses. If your bravery needs a little boost, check out the life stories of these champions of character and courage:

**Susan Boyle** was a seemingly ordinary, middle-aged British lady who lived with her cat and volunteered at her church. She ended up with multiple multi-million dollar offers, nearly 100 million views on YouTube and praise from across the globe five minutes after appearing on *Britain's Got Talent*. From relative obscurity to an international star with millions of albums sold worldwide, and two Grammys. She even performed for the

Queen of England after conquering her fear of appearing on stage in front of an audience larger than her church parish.

**Legson Kayira** was an African boy who grew up in the 1940s. He was born to parents so poor they couldn't afford to care for a child. Tired of carrying him, his mother decided to throw him into the river. Saved by a neighbor who found him before he drowned, he grew up named Didimu. After learning to read and write, he changed his name. Legson had one of the most difficult childhoods a kid could face, but the school he attended had a motto: "I will try." He adopted that motto as his own, allowing it to fuel him through the hard times in his life. After being rejected by a teacher's training school, a dream was born in his heart to go to college in the United States. At the age of 16, his dream set him on a two-year journey walking from Northern Malawi across 3,000 miles of Africa, through 4 countries, learning multiple languages along the way to arrive in Khartoum where he was given a visa and passage to the United States. Legson not only received a full scholarship to college but also went on to complete his masters before becoming an acclaimed author. He published his autobiography titled, "I Will Try" landing him on the New York Times bestseller list for 16 weeks followed by 5 more published novels.

A hero is no braver than an ordinary man, but he is braver five minutes longer.
–Ralph Waldo Emerson

**Stephen Cannell** overcame dyslexia to become an award-winning Hollywood scriptwriter.

**Rick Hoyt** was a quadriplegic man who overcame his disabilities to become a 4-time Ironman athlete.

**Jack Canfield** and **Mark Victor Hansen**, authors of

*Chicken Soup for the Soul,* received 134 rejections before getting their work published, becoming a best-seller, and then a series, and now a multi-faceted franchise.

**Andy Hensel** became the first quadriplegic in the world to do a backflip on a dirt bike.

**Tom Monaghan** was an entrepreneur who went from broke to founding Domino's Pizza.

Brazilian **Derek Rabelo** was born blind, but despite it, he learned to surf and became a professional surfer. A documentary about his life has encouraged many aspiring surfers and individuals worldwide.

**Baxter Humby** is the only kick boxer who has ever won a world title with only one hand. He also served as Tobey McGwire's stunt double in *Spider-Man 3*.

> You will not always be strong, but you can always be brave.
> –Beau Taplin

Each of these stories underscore one truth that is critical to living the Sweet Life: It's not the size of your obstacles that determine your life, but the size of your bravery! So, be courageous!

## The Four Components of Bravery

If you haven't drunk from your cup of courage lately or, worse yet, don't even know where to start, don't despair. Bravery can be learned. Here are the four components you need to increase your bravery quotient:

**FAITH:** To live the Sweet Life, you must understand the crippling power of fear and the insurmountable power of faith. Fear is a force, and faith is a force. You must choose which one you are going to submit to. You can either choose to live in fear and shrink back from life or choose to live by faith and expand your life. Your life will always accommodate whichever choice you make. Adopt a paradigm of bravery instead of a paradigm of fear. Be pro-bravery. To overcome fear and live in faith, you must believe in who God is and who He says you are. Allow His truth to become more real than any fear you feel.

**ACTION:** Do the hard thing: Take action. Fear, procrastination, and resistance will try to keep you in the safe, comfortable zone of average living. But, sweet friend, you were called to live the Sweet Life. The road to bravery isn't going to be comfortable. Get comfortable being uncomfortable. Take decisive action forward to defeat your fears. One of my favorite Bible heroes, David, was a man of action. He didn't just talk about the hard thing; he pursued the hard thing.

> *But David said to Saul, "Your servant has been keeping his father's sheep. When a lion or a bear came and carried off a sheep from the flock, I* **went after it,** *struck it and rescued the sheep from its mouth. When it turned on me, I seized it by its hair, struck it and killed it. Your servant has killed both the lion and the bear; this uncircumcised Philistine will be like one of them, because he has defied the armies of the living God. The Lord who rescued me from the paw of the lion and the paw of the bear will rescue me from the hand of this Philistine." … So it was, when the Philistine arose and came and drew near to meet David, that David* **hurried and ran toward** *the army to meet the Philistine. —1 Samuel 17:34-37, 48, NKJV (emphasis mine)*

David didn't run from an attack or a battle; he ran toward it. What battle have you been running from that you need to be running toward with the strength and confidence God has given you to defeat it?

Practice being brave—right where you're at and with whatever you're facing. Just like David, your little acts of bravery today will prepare you for even larger acts of bravery and eventually greater victories tomorrow. Bravery begets bravery. And remember, God has already won the battle for you, so your ability to be brave is simply your act of agreement with that truth.

**RISK:** Being brave means you won't have every detail figured out before you step out of the boat, so you can't be afraid to fail. Too many times we refuse to risk, second guess ourselves, and stay in our comfort zones. We worry about what the critics might say if we make a mistake or fall on our faces. I've had my fair share of epic failures and agonizing mistakes. But each of them made me stronger and more knowledgeable the next time I stepped out. Think of a recent situation when you took a risk and made a mistake. What did you learn? Mistakes don't define you; they develop you.

Trust the still, small voice that says, "this might work and I'll try it.
–Beau Taplin

If you're going to do anything big in life, you're going to make mistakes, but don't give ear to the critics. Read the words of Theodore Roosevelt—the 26th president of the United States and the youngest to hold the office up to that point—to gain a little perspective on why critics, naysayers, and negative Nancies don't count.

*It is not the critic who counts: not the man who points out how the strong man stumbled or where the doer of deeds could have done them better. The credit belongs to the man who is actually in the arena; whose face is marred by dust and sweat and blood; who strives valiantly; who errs, and comes short again and again, because there is no effort without error and short-coming; who does actually try to do the deed; who knows the great enthusiasm, the great devotion and spends himself in a worthy cause; who, at the worst, if he fails, at least fails while daring greatly.*

*Far better it is to dare mighty things, to win glorious triumphs even though checked by failure, than to rank with those poor spirits who neither enjoy nor suffer much because they live in the gray twilight that knows neither victory nor defeat.*

Those who try to tell you you'll never succeed or try to convince you that you're not qualified or smart enough are agents sent by the enemy to discourage your dreams. Don't buy into their message of mediocrity. It's meant to keep you small. Their empty words are just that—empty—devoid of power to define your destiny. Walk in the truth of your biggest cheerleader, the Holy Spirit within you. He will always speak a word of victory to your heart.

**FIGHT:** Most professional boxing fights that you see on television are rarely won in the first round. Boxers are trained to go round after round, trained to take a licking but keep on ticking. If you're going to be brave, you must learn to persevere in the face of adversity. Remember, if it was easy, everyone would do it.

It's not the size of the dog in the fight, it's the size of the fight in the dog.
–Mark Twain

I can remember when I started writing this book. I envisioned completing it in 6–8 months. Had I known then all of the things I would go through *(check out my journey on the next page)* and that it would take me just under four years to complete, I might have quit. But I determined to fight for my dream, and it was totally worth the perseverance. And you should contend for your calling too!

# What I thought my journey would look like

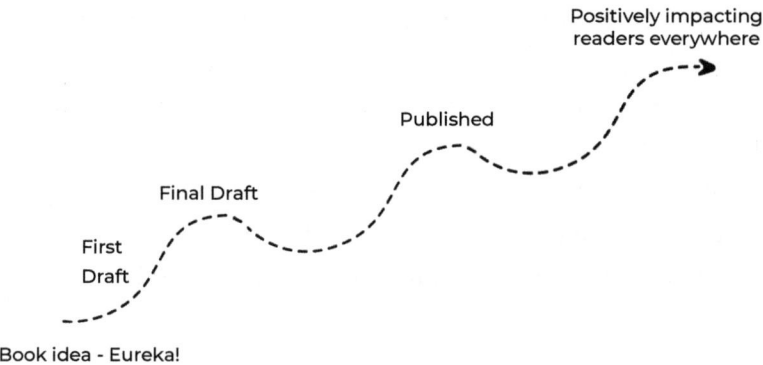

Positively impacting readers everywhere

Published

Final Draft

First Draft

Book idea - Eureka!

# What my journey actually looked like

*(and this is the paired down version!)*

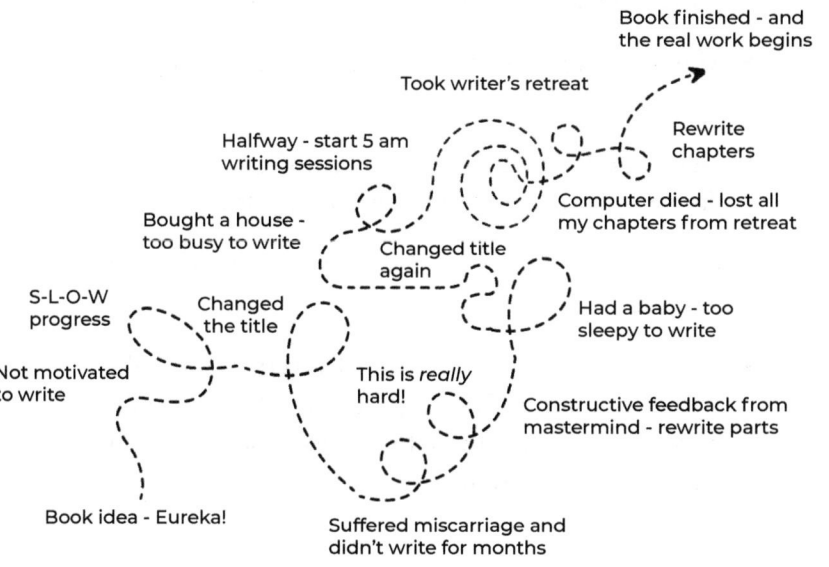

Book finished - and the real work begins

Took writer's retreat

Rewrite chapters

Halfway - start 5 am writing sessions

Computer died - lost all my chapters from retreat

Bought a house - too busy to write

Changed title again

S-L-O-W progress

Changed the title

Had a baby - too sleepy to write

Not motivated to write

This is *really* hard!

Constructive feedback from mastermind - rewrite parts

Book idea - Eureka!

Suffered miscarriage and didn't write for months

Here's what you will find to be true when pursuing the Sweet Life—things worth having take faith, grit, determination, patience, and endurance. The Bible encourages us not to get weary in well-doing, for in due season we will reap if we faint not (Galatians 6:9). Learn how to fight without fainting. You might get tired and need a break. Rest if you must for a moment, but jump right back in the fight. Your reward is on the other side of your resolve.

Work on these four components and you'll be on your way to becoming a gutsy girl who has mastered her moxie. Now go out there and be your best and bravest self!

## Sweet Life Secrets

- To live the Sweet Life, you must understand the crippling power of fear and the insurmountable power of faith. Fear is a force, and faith is a force.

- You must choose which one you are going to submit to.

- Get comfortable being uncomfortable. Take decisive action forward to defeat your fears.

- Remember, mistakes don't define you, they develop you.

- Learn to persevere in the face of adversity and fight without fainting. You might get tired and need a break. Rest if you must for a moment, but jump right back in the fight.

# The Queen Bee in Me

*In every woman, there is a Queen.*
*Speak to the Queen and the Queen will answer.*
*–Norwegian Proverb*

**BEE FACT**

A healthy honeybee colony has three distinct types of individuals: queen, worker, and drone. The queen is an especially important individual in the colony, as she is the only actively reproductive female and generally lays all the eggs.

Growing up as a little girl, I loved a good fairy tale. I loved reading tales of Snow Queens, fairy princesses, glass slippers, and magical kingdoms. What was even more fun was dressing up in one of my pretty dresses and playing the role of the queen. We didn't have the big poofy tutu dresses back in my day, but clothed in one of my nicer dresses reserved for church, I was transformed into a beautiful queen ruling over her kingdom. My upper bunk bed, piled high with pillows and blankets, served as my magical castle.

In my imaginative production, my four siblings each got a role. I dubbed them my servants and charged them to wait on me hand and food and do my bidding. Occasionally I opted to make them peasants and farmers in the village. Of course, that was as disastrous as it sounds; it never went over well with them. There was generally an uprising within the first few minutes as one of my sisters or brothers naturally wanted their opportunity to rule the throne. Usually, we would settle on three queens and two kings ruling side by side to save the kingdom from fierce dragons, invading armies, roaming bandits, and whatever else our young minds could dream up. One thing was certain: I liked being a queen. Even as a girl, my love of leadership was baked into my personality, and I wanted to be a wise, good queen.

## Long Live the Queen

As little girls grow up, our desire to be a queen, to feel special, be cherished, and be loved doesn't leave us. Sadly, many of us let other people, the disappointments and hurts of life, and the lies of the enemy into our hearts, causing us to forget our royal birthright and doubt our queenly value. If that's you, I can relate.

Before I discovered the queen bee God placed within me, I let insecurities about my image, bad relationships, and the devil's accusations and lies rob me of my royal identity. Instead of operating from a place of worth, I went searching *for* worth. This is a trick of the enemy and I'm here to remind you of the queen *you already are.*

All kings and queens are not born of royal bloodlines. Some become royal because of what they do once they realize who they are.
–Pharrell Williams

You needn't don a tiara or have a court of ladies in waiting to live royally. You simply need to live regally, making a positive effect on those around you. After all, you are a daughter of the King of Kings and a member of the royal family. You are called to reign in your own Sweet Life. It's time to rock your royalty.

## Heroines and Highnesses

The Bible is filled with queens—both those that left a positive mark and those that could give any wicked queen in a fairytale a run for their money. Most widely known are Queen Esther, the Queen of Sheba, and Queen Jezebel. From Bible times to present day, queens have made an impact. Historically, monarchies existed to provide order. They played a central role in the national unity and economic, political, and cultural framework of society. While you may not physically live in a castle or wear a jeweled crown on your head, that doesn't make your royal worth any less. Listen to what God has to say about your royal identity:

*"But you are a chosen people, a royal priesthood, a holy nation, God's special possession, that you may declare the praises of him who called you out of darkness into his wonderful light." - Peter 2:9*

I love that God spelled it out so clearly. You are royalty, and you're special to God. You are called to reflect His wonderful light in this world, so shine baby shine! Here's another one of my favorite passages on our supreme significance to the King of Kings:

*"You will be a crown of splendor in the LORD's hand, a royal diadem in the hand of your God." -Isaiah 62:3*

A diadem is a type of crown, an ornamental headband worn by monarchs and others as a badge of royalty. You are God's badge of royalty on the Earth.

Every day, you must choose to align your view of yourself with what God says about you, to operate out of this identity instead of from the pauper-and-peasant lies Satan works to convince you of. Satan will try to sell you the lie that you're forgotten, condemned, worthless, and a failure; whereas, God says you are cherished, forgiven, more than a conqueror, and so priceless you're worth the blood of His son. Refuse the poisoned apple of defeat the enemy is serving up and instead reclaim your crown.

Here are six ways you can live like the queen bee you are:

**1. Own your birthright.** You have been given a royal birthright as daughter of the King of Kings and you must learn to operate out of that identity. Even if you've messed up royally (pun intended), your past mistakes, failures, and flaws don't invalidate your claim to the crown. Decide today to accept all the heavenly heritage you have been given and walk as a beloved child of God.

Here's a Sweet Life exercise for you: Search out all the things God says you are in the Bible and write them down to create your own "I Am" list. My "I Am" list, in part, reads a little something like this: *I am loved, accepted, cherished, forgiven, chosen, declared righteous, honored, respected, celebrated, empowered, and equipped to be all that God has called me to be.*

Once you have your "I Am" list, post it in a place you will see it daily—your bathroom mirror or your desk at work. Then, pray and ask God to renew your mind to this new identity and to remind you what He says about you when the enemy tries to distract you with a lie. Spend time with Him and study out His promises until it becomes second nature for you to think and live like the royal diadem you are.

**2. Lead with love.** The queen models a life of service to others. In a world of brokenness, pain, and suffering, she carries out her duties in a spirit of love, humility, compassion, and gentleness. Be leaderly. Know your power, strengths, and

# My "I Am" List

*I Am:*

_____

_____

_____

_____

_____

_____

_____

_____

_____

_____

_____

**THESE ARE SOME OF MY ANSWERS:**

*I am loved, accepted, cherished, forgiven, chosen, declared righteous, honored, respected, celebrated, empowered, and equipped to be all that God has called me to be.*

talent and wield them for the good of others. A queen is loved by the people because she models a life of love for the people.

**3. Walk in conduct worthy of the crown.** Your conduct and sweet spirit can set a standard of excellence and grace for those around you. Look for ways to take your habits, thoughts, speech, and responses to a royal level. Instead of criticizing, can you praise, encourage, and pray? Instead of complaining, can you take action to implement a solution? A queen's not out telling others what to do (that's a tyrant). Instead, she's advising, guiding, and being a splendid role model, displaying her own quiet dignity while helping others achieve their full potential. You represent the King of Kings, so walk worthy of the crown. Let the rich, royal fruit of the Holy Spirit be cultivated in your life, attitude, and actions for all to see and enjoy.

> There's nothing so kingly as kindness, and nothing so royal as truth.
> –Alice Cary

**4. Elevate your daily routine.** Take everything in your life to a royal level. I'm not talking about spending a fortune, but do invest as needed injecting excellence into the details of your life and routine.

When the Queen of Sheba traveled to meet King Solomon and test him with hard questions, she not only left impressed by his wisdom, but also by the excellence of everything in his daily life. In fact, the Bible records in 1 Kings 10:1-9 that she was wowed to the point of being overwhelmed:

> *When the queen of Sheba heard about the fame of Solomon and his relationship to the Lord, she came to test Solomon with hard questions. Arriving at Jerusalem with a very great caravan—with camels carrying spices, large quantities of gold, and precious stones—she came to*

*Solomon and talked with him about all that she had on her mind. Solomon answered all her questions; nothing was too hard for the king to explain to her. When the queen of Sheba saw all the wisdom of Solomon and the palace he had built, the food on his table, the seating of his officials, the attending servants in their robes, his cupbearers, and the burnt offerings he made at the temple of the Lord, she was overwhelmed.*

*She said to the king, "The report I heard in my own country about your achievements and your wisdom is true. But I did not believe these things until I came and saw with my own eyes. Indeed, not even half was told me; in wisdom and wealth you have far exceeded the report I heard. How happy your people must be! How happy your officials, who continually stand before you and hear your wisdom! Praise be to the Lord your God, who has delighted in you and placed you on the throne of Israel. Because of the Lord's eternal love for Israel, he has made you king to maintain justice and righteousness.*

What in your life could use a royal upgrade? Can you ditch the plastic dishes, and instead of waiting for a special occasion, go ahead and enjoy the fine china? Are you eating like a peasant existing off fast food rather than treating your royal temple to the healthiest fare? Forgo the fries and take time out of your busy day to prepare nutritious food that will provide the fuel you need to thrive on the throne. Are you taking time to dress your best and

The king's daughter is all glorious within: Her clothing is interwoven with gold.
–Psalms 45:13, NASB

present a polished appearance? Do you need to care for yourself a bit better and schedule a regular manicure or pedicure or maybe

# Notable Queens that Changed the World

 ## Queen Esther

Esther was a Jewish queen of Persian descent. She came into her queendom after King Ahasuerus banished his first wife Vashti for refusing to appear before him and his drunken friends in the royal court. A national beauty pageant was created to choose the next queen. Enthralled by her beauty, King Ahaserus chose Esther to be queen out of all the women in the kingdom. Later when a plot to kill all the Jews was set into motion by the king's chief advisor Haman, Esther fasted for three days with all her maidens. Then she bravely risked her life by appearing before the king without invitation, requesting his presence at a banquet. At the banquet, the king offered to grant her any request, and she boldly revealed Haman's wicked plans, requesting that the Jews be able to fight back against their attackers. Esther, led by her faith in God, saved the entire Jewish nation. The King issued a royal decree protecting the Jews and demanding Hamaan's execution.

 ## Elizabeth I

Known as the Virgin Queen, Elizabeth I reigned over England during the Elizabethan era. Red-haired, white-faced, and fashionably dressed, she was known for her shrewd courage and majestic display. She believed herself to be wedded to the country and inspired passionate loyalty from the people. Under her rule, she famously defeated the Spanish Armada in 1588, unified the nation, and ushered in half a century of stability and prosperity.

###  Queen Elizabeth II

This queen is the longest reigning monarch in British history and the longest serving female head of state in world history. Queen over the United Kingdom, its realms and territories, and Head of the Commonwealth, Elizabeth II modernized many aspects of the monarchy. She traveled frequently, devoted her life to public service, and received the admiration of her people.

###  Queen Isabella

Isabella I married Ferdinand II of Aragon, unifying Spain. She financed the expedition of Christopher Columbus, leading to the discovery of the Americas. She also completed the Reconquista expanding the Christian kingdoms.

###  Queen Victoria

Lively and warmhearted, Victoria was queen of the United Kingdom and Ireland, ruling for 63 years, the second longest reign in British history. She is most noted for ushering in the Victorian era, a time of great scientific, industrial, political, and military change, establishing the South Kensington museum complex in London, and the expansion of the British kingdom. At her death, it was said, Britain had a worldwide empire on which the sun never set.

###  Cleopatra

Cleopatra was an Egyptian queen who served as co-regent for three decades. Although she ruled first with her father, and later with her two younger brothers and finally with her son, she was the dominant ruler in each regency, increasing Egypt's wealth and power during her reign. Well-educated, smart, and known for her legendary beauty and irresistible charm, she spoke over a dozen languages and shrewdly formed military alliances and infamous liaisons with Julius Cesar and Mark Antony.

 ## Joan of Arc

Born a peasant girl in France, Joan of Arc believed God spoke to her and chose her to help Charles the VII become king and lead France to victory in the Hundred Year War with England. With no military experience, she convinced the then-crowned Prince Charles to let her lead an army to battle in Orleans, defeating the English and French enemies there and winning many other momentous victories. Charles was soon crowned King, but years later Joan was caught by enemy forces, tried for witchcraft, heresy, and dressing like a man and was burned at the stake. Regarded as a heroine of France and an enduring symbol of French unity and nationalism, she was later canonized as a saint.

 ## Queen Bertha of Kent

Bertha was born a Frankish princess in 539. She agreed to marry Æthelberht, the pagan King of Kent, becoming queen, on the condition she be allowed to practice her faith in Christ. She arrived at Kent with a chaplain and established St. Martin's as her own private chapel (later becoming the first church founded in England). Years later, the queen aided in the conversion of her husband to Christianity—the first Anglo-Saxon king ever to do so. Known for her faith in Christ, her influence also helped prepare the way for St. Augustine to preach the gospel in England. Bertha passed down her godly influence and great spiritual legacy to her children and grandchildren, who continued in the faith throughout their generations.

give yourself the luxury of an earlier bedtime and enjoy a few more zzz's? After all, a snappy, sleep-deprived sovereign does not a queen make. Take stock of your life and determine what about your daily routine needs to be "queened up!"

**5. Stay Kingdom-minded.** The kingdom you rule is more than what you see with your eyes and what makes sense to your mind. As a daughter of God, you are seated in heavenly places with Christ and must operate with a different perspective and from a different place of power. Your dominion has been given through the strength of God's rule and authority to empower you to make an eternal impact in your life, family, culture, and spheres of influence. Make sure you're building God's kingdom and not just your own empire. God wants us to flourish and prosper in this life, but we must do it for His glory and to accomplish His purpose for this world.

> But seek ye first the kingdom of God, and his righteousness; and all these things shall be added to you.
> —Matthew 6:33, NKJV

**6. Take up your royal mission; seize your monarch moment.** Hear ye, hear ye, you have been henceforth and forevermore chosen by God for a royal mission! You have been placed on this earth to be a light-bearer, standard-raiser, love-giver, and world-changer. It's no mistake that God created you for this exact time in history. You were carefully crafted in your mother's womb for such a time as this. This is your monarch moment. It's your time to step out in faith and speak up as God grants you open doors and opportunities in the work He has uniquely called you to do.

For me, that calling is motivating and inspiring women to embrace their true identity, tap into their God-given potential, and have the kind of impact that they are capable of having in the world. What has He called you to do? Find a cure for disease, help address homelessness, bring people comfort with redesigned home interiors, or champion truth and justice in legislation? Whatever your cause, calling, or community, it's time to be bold and be about your queenly business! Rise up, Queen Esther. Rise up, Queen of Sheba. Rise up, Sweet Life Queen. It's time. It's *your time*!

> For if you remain silent at this time, relief and deliverance will arise for the Jews from another place and you and your father's house will perish. And who knows whether you have not attained royalty for such a time as this?
> –Esther 4:14, NASB

When you know Whose you are and who you are, you can walk in your royal heritage and begin to see the impact you can make all around you. Then, you're on track to being the sovereign of your own Sweet Life.

And as they say—it's good to be queen!

## Sweet Life Secrets

- You have been given a royal birthright as daughter of the King of Kings, and you must learn to operate out of that identity.

- Know your power, strengths, and talent and wield it for the good of others.

- Take everything in your life to a royal level by injecting excellence into the details of your life and routine.

- Make sure you're building God's kingdom and not just your own empire. God wants us to flourish and prosper in this life, but we must do it for His glory and to accomplish His purpose for this world.

- Seize your monarch moment. Step out in faith and speak up as God grants you open doors and opportunities to do the work He has uniquely called you to do.

# Acknowledgements

God, thank You, above all else, for showing me that the Sweet Life was Your idea all along and inviting me to experience it with You daily.

To my mother and father, Charles and Sandra Reed, and siblings, Titus, Anna, and Ben—no one has played a greater role in this book becoming a reality than you all. Your persistent faith in me and untiring encouragement to *"keep going"* are the reason this books is a reality. Special thanks to Anna—for talking me back into the light when my computer died and I lost all the chapters I wrote during my writers retreat and for not holding me to my promise when I bet a sizable sum of money that I could finish the book within sixty days but failed miserably.

Sarah Jewel, you mean the world to me and my Sweet Life is not complete without you.

Chris and Gena Maselli of Writing Momentum (writingmomentum.com)—this book could not have happened without your skills, guidance, and brilliant editing.

To Ryan and Ellie Binkley for showing me the generational blessing of living the Sweet Life.

To my Create family, thank you for a life-giving hive to call home.

My deepest gratitude and appreciation for my Sweet Life girlfriends, you know who you are. Thank you for being my tribe and cheering on my dreams. As iron sharpens iron, thank you for refining this book and the principles within over countless coffee chats, brunch brainstorms, accountability phone calls, and persistent prayers through the years.

To my mom-in-love, Gloria, thank you for encouraging me to have a regular quiet time. So much of this book was birthed in those moments.

Llewellyn, my forever love—your affirmation, belief, prayers, and confidence in me are the greatest gifts. Thank you for always pushing me to pursue my pasions, even when it takes time away from the family. I'm so blessed to share this bee-utiful life with you.

Aiden, my precious son—may wisdom, like honey, be sweet to your soul all the days of your life, so that you experience the rewarding future and eternal hope God has promised you.

Lastly, thanks to every woman who aspires to walk in the fullest expression of who God created you to be. I believe in you. You can do it. With grit and grace, let's go!

# About the Author

Ruth Jones is an author, speaker, life and brand strategist, and creative entrepreneur. Ruth owns a company whose mission is to empower people to embrace their true identity, maximize their God-given potential, and have the kind of impact that they are capable of having in the world. With radiant positivity and thought-provoking wit, she uses her writing to challenge you to smash through your limitations and experience a life of possibility and dream-fulfillment. Ruth makes her home in Dallas, Texas, with her husband, Lou, and rambunctious son, Aiden.

@ruthjonesinspires

@ruthinspires

/ruthjonesinspires

@ruthjonesinspires

ruthjonesinspires.com

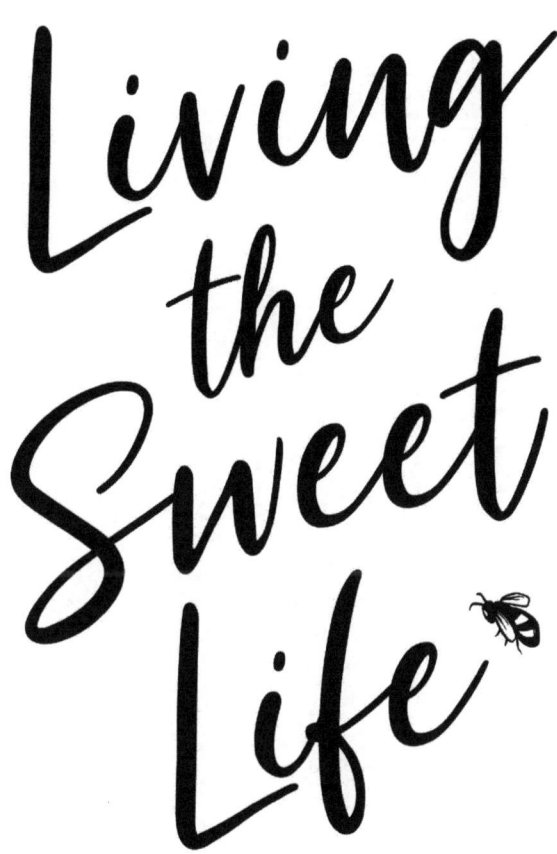

STAY ENGAGED with
*Living the Sweet Life* and Ruth Jones

#SweetLife

ruthjonesinspires.com

Milton Keynes UK
Ingram Content Group UK Ltd.
UKHW021344090824
1219UKWH00040B/266